TALES OF SOUTHERN RIVERS

FISHING BOOKS BY
ZANE GREY

TALES OF FISHES

TALES OF SOUTHERN RIVERS

TALES OF FRESH–WATER FISHING

TALES OF FISHING VIRGIN SEAS

TALES OF SWORDFISH AND TUNA

TALES OF THE ANGLER'S ELDORADO,
NEW ZEALAND

WATERFALL ON A TROPICAL RIVER

TALES OF SOUTHERN RIVERS

by

Zane Grey

Author of "Tales of Fishes,"
"Tales of Fishing Virgin Seas," etc.

With Many Illustrations
from Photographs

GROSSET & DUNLAP
Publishers : : New York

TALES OF SOUTHERN RIVERS

CONTENTS

LIST OF ILLUSTRATIONS

vii

LIST OF ILLUSTRATIONS

LIST OF ILLUSTRATIONS

ix

THE GREAT RIVER OF THE GULF

THE GREAT RIVER OF THE GULF

I

IT may be something of a poetic fallacy to call the Gulf Stream a river of the South, a flowing stream within the sea, but to me that is just what it is. As a matter of fact it is a current of blue water fifty miles or more wide, and it moves appreciably faster than the green ocean water that it divides.

This dark blue river is a thing of beauty and mystery. It circles the Gulf of Mexico, flows up the straits between the Bahama Islands and Florida, and, gradually working away from the coast, it passes north, carrying to colder shores some of the beneficent warmth of the South.

Off Long Key, Florida, on approaching the Gulf Stream from the reef there can be seen a chafing of the waters, a long line of low whitecaps and blue water encroaching upon the green. The air becomes more balmy, and, once in the Stream, the several degrees of higher temperature can be appreciated. The current flows north and seems to be quite swift, though to the best of my calculations it moves only several miles an hour. The prevailing winds are the northeast trades, and blowing quarterly against this current they usually kick up a choppy sea. Short, billowy, white-crested swells, rough on boat and angler!

On a fine day, with just the right breeze, the Gulf Stream presents a changing, beautiful panorama of blue and white rolling waters. It breathes of the tropics, blowing fragrance from far-off palm-bordered shores, and laden with the lonely atmosphere of coral reefs. It does not seem like the sea, except in motion. It apparently has nothing in common with the green-blanched, restless Atlantic main. It flows from under the Equator, with the message of unplumbed tropic seas. Its depth and current, its mystery and charm, its burden of marine life, will ever be a fascinating study for naturalists.

One of the strangest of its creations is the Portuguese man-of-war. This is a small sea creature, some form of fish life, a tiny six-inch balloon of blue or lilac, with a corrugated crest, and numerous long threads or feelers, dark violet in hue. It blows, like a miniature ship, where the wind listeth. The natives of these coral reefs will show a small curled blue shell, fragile and delicate, from which they claim the Portuguese man-of-war is born, somewhere out at sea. I doubt this, but be that as it may, the little vessels can be seen any warm day sailing out their destinies on the deep. Always they seem to be blowing from the other side of the Gulf Stream. In calm water they appear to have some little control over their locomotion. I have seen one stand on end, turn over, and reverse himself, a singular action, the utility of which was not manifest. They make little shining colored dots on the blue sea. The only enemy they have, so far as I can learn, is the loggerhead turtle.

Every Portuguese man-of-war has one or more, sometimes half a dozen, of exquisite little fish that for want of a known name I call butterfly fish, for their striking resemblance to a blue and silver winged insect. These little fish attend the Portuguese man-of-war on his drifting des-

tiny toward the sand. Both are marked for tragedy. The
Portuguese man-of-war drifts to the shore, is deserted by
his strange comrades, and is cast up on the beach to die,
and become food for the ghost-crabs. It would be good
to think that the butterfly fish find another protector, but
I cannot be convinced of this. Many miles they have
traveled together, in some affinity as strange as beautiful;
and it is a long perilous way back to the depths of the
Gulf Stream. I rather imagine the little butterfly fish are
lost on the shoals, prey to innumerable keen-eyed enemies.
Assuredly they have no defense, once they have parted
from the Portuguese man-of-war. The long six-foot feelers
of this sea creature secrete a poisonous substance that is
paralyzing to the flesh of man, and probably equally so to
fish. Perhaps the butterfly fish find their protection inside the radius of these long feelers.

The winter of 1924 was noted all over the south and
west as being one of unusually bad weather. At Long
Key for days there had been unsettled weather, southwest
winds, and northwesters, and finally the genuine *del norte*.
One day was very cold. Then for two days the wind lulled
at noon, and the afternoons grew calm and warm. At last
the wind made a little shift toward northeast.

I went out to the Gulf Stream one morning; cool, in-
vigorating, with the sun not too bright, and the sea just
ridged with white. We headed for Half Moon Reef, and
trolled across it hoping to catch a mackerel for bait. But
we were not so fortunate. We went on into the Stream.

It did not seem as blue as usual, which was owing, no
doubt, to the reflection of sky. The sea grew somewhat
rough, then gradually went down with the breeze. I
trolled a cut bait of mullet, not overly fresh, and it was a

long time until I had a strike. I saw the sailfish. He looked big and bronze. He let go, then came back, took the bait with a swoop, and shot away. I let him run. I was using 6-9 tackle, and handled it accordingly. I hooked this fish. He ran a long way without leaping. When he circled we ran to meet him. Then he swerved toward us, and I could not get in the slack, though I wound the reel with might and main. We could not locate him; and at last when I saw the line going under the boat, it was too late. He leaped on the other side, a big sailfish, with his sail spread. The line had a lot of slack and it floated up on the swells, before I could reel in, and it fouled on the boat. We tried to poke it loose, but finally had to break it and pull up the other part with a gaff and break that. Then we tied the ends together. The sailfish was still on. I worked him toward the boat, to find that he was keeping company with several others. Here the hook pulled out. All our trouble had been in vain. The other sailfish disappeared.

This was a bad start. It augured ill. We went on. A little later I saw a white fish about two feet long darting toward the stern. It was a huge remora, and he was evidently making for the boat to attach himself to it, perhaps taking it for a fish. The remora species has a flat disk on top of its head, an arrangement of suckers, and with these he clings to the fish he lives upon. The remora, sucking-fish, shipholder, pilot fish, are all one and the same, although there are many varieties. Seldom is a sailfish or shark or swordfish caught that does not have one or more of these little parasites on him, often in the gills.

Presently I espied the sharp spear-pointed tails of sailfish riding the swells. We ran close to discover a large

HOUSEBOAT "LADYFISH"

SAILFISH TUMBLING

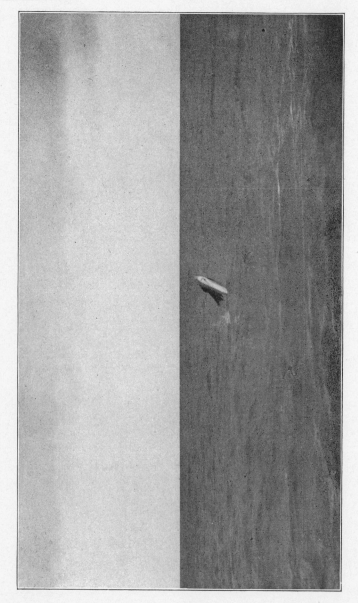

A LEAPING SAILFISH

school.   They always work south against the Gulf Stream
current.   I never saw a sailfish swimming or leaping any
way except against the current.   We crossed in front of
them, and I had a strike.   I hooked this one, and he
came out at once, throwing the hook.   My bad start
was holding on.   We chased the school and got in front
of them again.   I could see the slim smooth bronze backs
cutting the water, and the sickle tails coming out of the
swells.   Soon I had three or four after my bait; and one
got away with it.   We lost this school before we could
get out another bait.

In the succeeding hours I sighted three more large
schools.   And I hooked five more fish, only one of which
I got to the boat.   We fooled a good deal with several,
trying to make them leap for pictures.   Otherwise I might
have caught one or two more.   Late in the afternoon I
hooked a large wahoo, and lost it, too.

This was one of the bad luck days, common to every
angler of wide experience.   It seemed inexplicable, considering that the other boats all caught sailfish, some of
them a number.   One woman who had never before caught
a sailfish got one weighing seventy-four and a half pounds,
a remarkable fish, eight feet two inches long.   A still
larger one was caught, measuring eight feet, six inches,
which is the longest recorded here.   Some of the boatmen reported dozens of schools of sailfish up toward Alligator Reef.   Here and there one of these schools refused
to notice a bait, but most of them were hungry.   There
was a big run of sailfish on at this time.   The territory
of the day ranged fully twenty miles.   Manifestly there
were more fish to the north than to the south, within this
limit.

This date was about the first quarter of the moon in February.

II

WE had a long spell of bad weather—northwesters, northers, northeasters, all the same as far as concerned wind. This Long Key coral reef lay between the Gulf of Mexico and the Atlantic Ocean; and it was no wonder the cocoanut trees seemed born to combat wind. How they leaned away from the northeast trade-wind! How they showed their struggle against the hurricane!

There came a day when at sunrise the sea was gently rippled, and there was scarcely any wind. I saw the first dull red gleam of the sun as it rose above the level horizon into a bank of purple cloud. This bank was a long line of trade-wind clouds, flat above its base, broken and columnar above. Soon these lofty edges began to take on the freshness of bright color—gold. Far up in the sky floated a sea of wispy particles of cloud, like blown feathers. They turned to silver. Soon there was a beautiful sunrise of gold and silver, without one vestige of the morning red.

Nevertheless, the wind came with the sunrise.

Not to be daunted, R. C. and I were the first to leave the dock; and in half an hour were bumping the heavy green seas of Hawk Channel. All the time the wind grew stronger. By the time we reached the Gulf Stream there was a rough sea running. We continued out into the dark blue tumbling waters and began to troll for sailfish.

The wind blew strong from the east; the tide appeared to be moving south and was unusually heavy; the current of the Gulf Stream headed north. Thus we breasted a cross sea of contending strife. It was very fascinating to watch, but most uncomfortable to endure.

What made the latter possible was the fact that sailfish began to loom up like bronze flashes behind our baits. One and two at a time would shoot aloft in a great blue swell and dart at our baits, only to pass them by. I was all a quiver with excitement at the chance of seeing a sail-fish leap aloft out of a white crested swell.

Flying fish rose from the seething water and sped like tiny steel hydroplanes over the billows. Something was chasing them. Several of the flying fish were no larger than humming birds; and one narrowly missed falling into the boat.

R. C. called my attention to sailfish swooping down the incline of a giant wave, under our lines, and between us and the baits. Then, as we were heaved higher and higher, I espied a fish larger than any I had seen, and of more vivid color, with the telltale purple that spelled Mar-lin swordfish. Like a flash he was gone.

The wind increased, and the sea likewise. I had not visited the Gulf Stream in such a surging turmoil. The water splashed all over us and the motion was so violent that we had to hold on. It became work, and most un-pleasant work. So soon I gave the word to head for Long Key Camp.

Whereupon we were to experience the relief and pleas-ure of a following sea. How the wonderful blue waves, mountains of water, raced after us, threatened to fall in blue ruin upon our boat, but instead lifted us like a feather and swept us forward in a motion of irresistible and gliding power! The propeller, lifted out of the water, roared its abrupt release from strain. Then down the billows we rode, rolled to larboard, rolled to starboard, until another giant rushed on us with mighty arms. Verily this day the great river of the Gulf seemed a terrible and devastating element of nature.

There followed days with cold westerly and northwest winds, and then the wind got back into the east.

Nevertheless, we ventured out to the reef. There was a tumultuous sea running, both high and shifting. The Gulf Stream was an impassable river for us this day. We got within two hundred yards of it—near enough to see the tremendous cross current and to hear the roar of contending tides. It was a beautiful wild sight, dark blue, white crested, chafing along against the bright green waters.

Sailfish showed in the transparent billows, long, slim, sharp, bronze fish, riding the swells and shooting down the curving slopes of the waves. We maneuvered the boat so that we got ahead of some of them, and drew our baits in front of their very bills. They would follow the baits awhile, then shoot on forward, to come even with the boat and to pass it, not ten feet distant. This afforded a wonderful opportunity to see the sailfish close at hand, free, indifferent to bait or boat. They had marvelous control over their native element, as much at home there as a frigate bird in the air.

We tried a number this way without getting a strike, and then decided it was one of their off days. Sometimes they will not touch any kind of bait, and at others they will bite anything.

The boat tossed like a cork upon the waves and the tips of the crests curled over into the cockpit, wetting us thoroughly. It was not possible to sit in the fishing seats without holding on; and at that the sudden jars and shocks, the tilting to one side, then to the other, were most uncomfortable and alarming.

Yet the great green billows, so exquisitely bright in the sunlight, fascinated me, and made me reluctant to start back to camp. Not often did we encounter a sea like that. It showed something of the unrest and hidden power of the ocean. The cloud shadows sailed like dark ships across the heaving plain of green. Now we were down in the trough, and anon lifted high upon a wave. Everywhere over the waves shone the little colored Portuguese men-of-war riding out the gale as if perfectly at home. How delicate these globules! Yet the whole might of the stormy main seemed powerless to destroy them. Many were accompanied by the tiny butterfly fish; and to see them together in that wild ocean was something beyond understanding. Both creatures seemed intended for shallow tranquil waters. Perhaps they blew across the Gulf Stream from the Cuban shoals. But my belief was that they came into being right there in the blue Stream.

At last we turned campward, and again had the exhilarating movement occasioned by a following sea. We were lifted high and higher, heaved aloft, driven forward and down, to the music of thunderous waves that threatened to engulf the boat, yet always passed on under us.

As far as Long Key was concerned, and elsewhere, so far as I knew, I was the first angler to take sailfish on light tackle. This was in 1916. Theretofore sailfish had been mostly caught while the angler was fishing for other surface fish.

My first tackle was a nine-ounce rod and fifteen-thread line. I used a wire leader and two hooks, and for bait half a mullet, or, better, a whole ballyhoo or white fish. We trolled at moderate speed, and when a sailfish took hold we let him run, sometimes, when he was wary, a long way, before hooking him. Sometimes when one tapped the bait we let it drift back to him, and if he took it and let go we gave him more line, until he took it for sure. I used to jerk the bait away from a finicky biter just to aggravate him.

This method brought results, though even then I realized it was not the right one. But at the time I could not improve upon it.

Sailfishing to-day has grown to be an art. The experts, a few, use a six-ounce tip and nine-thread line, which is a little light for heavy fish. One hook is used, a number eight, fastened on thin wire with an end left free to hold the head of the cut bait. (The illustrations show both hook and bait.) In trolling the speed is easily six or seven miles an hour, which is going pretty fast. Even then, sometimes a sailfish will refuse a bait. Cut bait of mullet is commonly used, but the best is a piece of bonita or mackerel belly. All the boatmen cut bait; but only the boatmen native to Florida, and used to cutting fish with a sharp knife, can do the trick with a most finished art. The proof is that a perfectly cut bait will attract a sailfish that will refuse one poorly cut. Captain Newton Knowles, of Miami, is one of the best bait-cutters I have ever known.

The small hook hangs perfectly and is scarcely felt. The method of procedure is, when the sailfish strikes, to let him run a few yards, then give him the rod hard. As to fighting a sailfish, I prefer to chase him when he is running and work on him, pump and wind, when he is sounding. This does not appear to be the general method in vogue at Long Key. All the boatmen, at least those I observed, ran round and round with the sailfish. In most instances fish caught by members of the club were not gaffed, but held by the bill and detached from the hook and released.

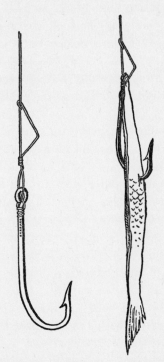

ILLUSTRATING THE USE OF THE CUT BAIT FOR SAILFISH

In a few cases, when a fish has been hooked in the corner of the mouth or the hard upper jaw, he may survive. But years of study and observation, and correspondence with ichthyologists have convinced me that the great majority —almost all of the fish returned alive to the water—are prey for sharks. It would be impossible to return an unhooked fish to the water without some blood scent emanating from the wound. And any student of sea fish knows what that means. It is infinitely more fatal than the trail of a crippled deer in the snow. For the ocean is a place of savage and unremittent strife.

I have come to the conclusion that to release fish, in most cases, is a mistake. "Liberated fish" is a high-sounding term, but it is only an excuse to go on catching more and more. What is almost as bad, it breeds dishonesty in that class of fishermen who wish to excel in number of fish caught. These anglers do not love fish for their beauty or gameness. Their fishing is a display of egotism. Clubs that reach the stage of intense competition for prizes and records are in danger and a record of seventeen sailfish released in one day is open to suspicion.

It seems difficult to offer a suitable remedy. A limit of one or two sailfish would not suit many anglers, for the simple reason that so few good days are possible, that when a fisherman happens on one he wants to catch as many sailfish as possible. If the fish caught were brought in and sold as at Avalon, or given away, even at the trifling expense of express rate to the nearest town, it would be a vastly commendable thing.

The use of teasers—baits or lures trolled behind the boat to attract sailfish—was first used by Avalon boatmen in Marlin fishing. I tried it at Long Key years ago, and pronounced it a failure because mackerel, barracuda, and other fish snapped off the cut-bait teasers as fast as they could be put out. The tarporeno wooden plug lure minus the hooks has taken the place of the destructible fish bait, and seems to work as well.

Sailfishing on light tackle comes very close to being the

finest sport of the trolling game.   And since the advent of
small Marlin swordfish at Miami and Long Key, such
angling has an added fascination.

III

EVERYTHING is emphasized by contrast.   The day I had
selected to fish from Sandy Key lighthouse, on the edge of
the Gulf Stream off Key West, to Sombrero Reef, turned
out to be surprisingly ideal.   Good weather was necessary
for fishing fifty miles of Gulf Stream, and this was almost
too good to be true.   After the everlasting gales and
northers and winds, what a relief and a joy to have a calm
day!

The sea was smooth, rippled by a slight breeze; and as
we ran out toward the stream crevalle were cracking the
green water in pursuit of ballyhoo.   The gulls and pelicans
were hovering aloft, swooping down now and then to
pounce upon a disabled fish.   Far out over the glistening
emerald sea showed the dark bulk of oil steamers on their
way to Tampico.

I could have wished for a little more wind, but, as there
appeared promise of some later on, I thought the day
might turn out perfect for fishing as well as comfort.

Long before we reached the Gulf Stream I saw the dark
line of blue water sharply defined against the green.   There
was now no ruffled current, as on windy days.   The cloudy
violet water merged irregularly into the green, raggedly
and mistily, with streamers and ribbons, and thick bulks
of solid color, and thin broken wandering lines.   A low,
heaving swell, just a perceptible movement of the water,
made me think of the Pacific.   And this was the only time

in my experience that the Atlantic Ocean ever reminded me of the Pacific. It added immeasureably to the thrill of the moment, to the prospect of the day.

Then in the green water just outside the Stream we saw two sailfish leap, a large one and a small one. Both came sliding out on their sides, in the graceful action characteristic of these fish. It looked like play to me. When sailfish leap to shake off the remoras they come out high and rather convulsively, and make several leaps, sometimes as many as nine or ten in succession.

We turned and ran ahead of where they had showed, and trolled out baits over the spot and all around it, to no avail. Then we headed into the Gulf Stream. I climbed out on the bow, leaving R. C. to do the trolling, and took a position facing north, so that I could command the water-level ahead. It seemed rather remarkable that I could actually have a comfortable seat on a launch in the Gulf Stream. But it was a most pleasant fact.

Several flying fish shot up from our bow and skimmed in different directions. They were larger than any I had seen in the Stream farther north. This was rather far south. So I watched for more flying fish. They did not appear plentiful. Yet in the course of a mile several more rose. I noted that as they came out their wings curved upwards, and as long as the lower lobes of their tails were propelling them towards the final sail, these wings fluttered, somewhat resembling wings of birds. Then when the flying fish cleared the water their wings straightened stiff, and held that position until they lowered their tails for more propulsion. They could cover a long stretch of water. It was conceivable for me that a flying fish might, in the process of evolution, really come to fly. In the

Pacific I have never seen either the curved or fluttering wings.

R. C. called out. I felt the boat slow to a released clutch, and, hurrying aft, I found R. C. jerking the light tackle hard, in the act of hooking a sailfish. I made a dive for the cameras and, placing them in good position on the seats, I took up one and stood beside my brother.

"He's a lunker," said R. C. as the line whizzed off. "There were two, and the bigger struck at the teaser . . . Cap, I guess you'd better chase this bird."

Whereupon we ran down on the sailfish. He came up, a goodly distance out, and leaped with the peculiar jerky action common to this species. He had no consistent way of coming out, though of course he always did so head first. But he was spasmodic and convulsive. Once he shot aloft, very high, waving his spread sail, and, turning a complete somersault, he plunged back. This was the kind of picture I always wanted to get of a leaping sailfish. On this particular leap I was winding up the camera. After nine or ten jumps he sounded, and worked away, swimming hard and fast. We chased him, headed him off, and R. C. endeavored to turn him back so he would run in the direction we wished to take. This appeared no easy matter. R. C. bent the little Murphy rod to an alarming extent.

Presently a yellow shape showed indistinctly in the violet water. I caught the motion. Shark! And he assuredly accomplished what R. C. could not—he started that sailfish north. Such a run! It was all of nine hundred feet. And we were hard put to it to keep up with him. Evidently he had eluded the shark, for he slowed down and kept plugging away, much to our satisfaction.

R. C. pumped and wound while we ran up on him. I was expecting a second series of leaps, if this sailfish acted normally, and, sure enough, was not disappointed.

He came out shining like a green-white and silvered bird with purple wings. And his next leap was a wiggling supple exhibition that reminded me of an action inspired by jazz music. Suddenly he became enraged, and threshed on the surface, and skittered toward us half out of water. This came as close to the Marlin's famous feat of walking on his tail as the less powerful sailfish could attain. He was not strong enough to raise himself all the way out and then go wagging across the sea in white boiling foam. But he gave a marvelous display of frantic motion of every kind, while all the while one-fourth of his body remained in the water. This might have lasted ten seconds or longer. I had no way to judge. It was a frenzied and strenuous energy, and took his stamina. I could see him growing weaker as both effort and distance of each separate motion lessened. Finally he made a last supreme effort, describing a parabolic dive, and then he soused back for good. I had made ten pictures of him during this brief sequence.

R. C. seemed disposed, as he always is unless incited to violence, to take it easy. So finally I said, "Time is passing. We can't hang around here all day to watch this sailfish swim. I'd like to look for some more fish."

"Uhuh! And hook me onto them!" declared R. C., still good-natured. But he proceeded to "wrap the hickory into him," as Captain Sid was wont to say on occasions, and brought the sailfish up to the boat.

One good look at this fish at close range convinced me I had been right about his being large. He was certainly the largest R. C. had ever hooked. So I advised careful handling, and in due time we pulled him into the boat, a beautiful specimen of iridescent colors. We estimated him at seventy pounds, but he would have weighed more, perhaps eighty. Owing to the many mistakes we had made in guessing the weight of fish, we had learned to underestimate.

I took up my rod and, standing in the cockpit, I fished while at the same time I kept a keen eye on the lookout for anything. That was the pleasure of such roaming the sea. Indeed, seldom in twelve winter seasons off Long Key had we ever had comfortable water, so that we could enjoy looking for sea creatures. We had been busy holding on to the boat to keep in it.

I saw a purple-and-pink jellyfish, a globular ethereal creature, moving with its own life as well as the current of the Stream. What an exquisite creature! I peered over to see more distinctly. It passed on, faded, and vanished. All I could remember was the rare color, the strange delicacy and abnormality of structure, the sucking bellows-like action that evidently propelled it, and the undoubtable fact of life. I had never before seen any other living thing like it and the chances were I never would again. Here is the fact that makes the ocean so supremely above all other mediums of nature, in fascinating possibilities, in unsolvable mysteries, in endless experiences.

I was just straightening erect, to go on looking for more things, when I had a ferocious strike. Whatever it was jerked the reel-spool from under my thumb and sent it spinning to a back-lash. Tangle! I felt the solid weight of a fish, and the break when he tore loose.

"Can't you see a fish?" queried my brother. "That one loomed up like a whale behind your bait."

"So? Well, what was it?" I returned.

"Looked to me like an enormous sailfish," he said, complacently.

I did not get any consolation from R. C., but presently I was revenged by seeing him miss as pretty a strike as an angler could wish for. I refrained from satire. A look about R. C. then inspired me to the hope that he had a hunch. As hunches are rather rare with him, I did not want to interfere, especially as they are apt to be auguries of good luck!

He scanned the smooth violet sea, out to the horizon line, and then back across the ragged mark where Stream and green water contended, and on to the dim white beaches and cocoanut palms of the lonely keys.

"Sometimes we go long before we hit it," he said. "I've a hunch it's going to be a day. One of our days! Look out!"

If I needed anything to rouse me to keener sense of possibilities, I had it in this from R. C. The sea had brightened with a glancing dark ripple and a more perceptible swell. The sun grew hot. White trade-wind clouds appeared off to the southwest, which really did not appear to be the right quarter for them. A huge oil tanker, magnified by the heat haze, bisected the level horizon line. I saw a leopard shark leap. He came out white and straight, turned clear over in the air, after the manner of all sharks when they leap to throw off parasites, and fell back to send up a great splash. I could judge something of his size by the amount of white water he raised. And five hundred pounds would not have been

an exaggeration. We crossed one of the clear green inlets that straggled into the blue Gulf Stream, and espied
another shark, this one a hammerhead of perhaps two
hundred pounds. He flashed yellow in the water, and
was a slim, fast, brutal-looking fish. I will always hook
up with such a rare and mean shark as this one, if it is
possible, and I directed the boatman to run round him so
that I could draw a bait close to him. R. C. recommended
the heavy tackle, which we always kept at hand, baited
and ready. I dragged a piece of mullet right across in
front of this shark, and he rushed it, nimble as a minnow,
ravenous as a tiger. When he sheered off I sat down,
jammed the rod in the socket, and gave him a real broad-
bill-swordfish strike.

"Wow! That's handin' it to 'em!" shouted R. C.
"Pull his head off!"

Manifestly my brother bore no more love for sharks
than I. In the scheme of nature I grant they were once
necessary to the balance of life in the ocean, but in the
light of the depletion of our salt-water fishes, by fleets of
net boats and other means, I believe some sharks can be
spared. Anyway, I welcome the shark industry that has
lately been started on both coasts, and think the results
of killing sharks will be beneficial.

This hammerhead probably was surprised at the sud-
denness with which he had been halted at his favorite
sport. With my swordfish tackle I felt I could do almost
as R. C. suggested. I shut down with both drags and
both thumbs, and hauled back with all my might. How
absurd to feel a sudden rage! But I did feel it, and I
stopped the hammerhead short. He wagged that strange,
cruel head, swirled on the surface, pounded the water with

great slaps, and struggled desperately. But I had him coming.

"Fine work! Pull his head off!" said R. C. cheerfully.

I pulled so hard that I pulled the hook out. After a moment's chagrin I regarded the matter as an incident of the fishing day, and went back to my lighter tackle.

From time to time I espied a loggerhead turtle on the surface. It was always fun to run down on them. They were exceedingly wary for such ungainly creatures. Every little while they lifted their huge blunt hawk-like heads to peer around. When they had their heads submerged it was easy to glide right upon them. Then they made frantic efforts to escape the looming monster above. Once started into motion, they disappeared very rapidly in the blue depths.

Next to attract us were the tiny flying-fish. They flitted up like steely locusts and glinted in the sunlight and darted away a few yards, to fall back. They had no control over direction. Once I saw one close to the boat and high enough to be silhouetted against the sky. He was scarcely two inches long. I discerned wings and tail, tiny black eye in a blunt little head. Except for that eye he appeared steely white in color. He popped out of a wave and blew with the gentle breeze.

Captain Knowles called our attention to sailfish leaping ahead. We looked eagerly, one on each side of the boat. I saw two sailfish come out at once in their long side leaps, some hundred yards ahead. One of them kept on leaping until he had seven jumps to his credit. Far beyond that point another leaped. Then we saw white splashes here and there.

SAILFISH WALKING ON HIS TAIL

SAILFISH NEAR BOAT

MOLA-MOLA, A SPECIES OF SUNFISH

"School of sailfish! Good night!" exclaimed R. C. "I'll eat my lunch!"

But he did not lay down his rod. Presently I saw a number of sharp dark tails piercing the surface and moving swiftly.

"Cross ahead of them, Cappy," I directed the boatman.

We let out line as the boat sheered, and soon saw the gleaming bronze figures of sailfish coming in great numbers. A school of any kind of game fish is always an inspiring sight. Sailfish in this school appeared to be as thick as fence pickets. Soon there were a dozen behind our baits.

"Pick out a big one," yelled R. C., maneuvering his bait. This was fun, even if it was impossible. The only thing we could do was to wind our baits in away from a small fish, but this only made that fish, and all the others, rush the baits harder. We both had strikes at once. R. C. hooked his quickly. I missed mine. He came back at the bait, took it again, let go, recovered it, and ran swiftly. I pulled it away from him. The third time he snatched it, made furious by the teasing. I let him go far, then hooked him.

Just then R. C.'s fish leaped high and crossed my line. We performed acrobatics to change positions and to pass my rod under his. The lines, speeding off the reels all the time, came straight. My sailfish took to pyrotechnics more in the air than in the water. R. C.'s ran off deep.

Meanwhile the boatman had been throwing the wheel over hard, so as to get in a position to chase our fish. We soon found ourselves surrounded by sailfish. They passed the boat on each side in an endless stream.

"Hey! Look at that son-of-a-gun biting my line!" yelled my brother.

It was indeed plain to see. A sailfish, not more than seventy feet out, had his mouth open like a scissors and was biting at the line. We had seen this before, but never so close. It was highly diverting for me, and I gayly instructed R. C. to pull the line away from the tricky fish. R. C. swore. Then he shouted for me to attend to my own troubles. It developed that I had some. Two sailfish, some fifteen feet apart, were operating on my line.

"Say, if you sailfish had any sense you'd saw the line off with your bills, instead of trying to bite it off," I remarked.

However what might have been, the fact was that the nearer sailfish quit, and the second fooled with my line until he cut it. I reeled in and began hurriedly to rig on another leader.

"Oh boy! Look at 'em jump!" ejaculated R. C.

And I had to give up my task to watch. We appeared to be in the midst of the school. R. C.'s victim had excited some of them and they were threshing, sliding, breaking on the surface. His fish was small, but he was a jumper. When he turned toward us, that was too much for me and I abandoned my tackle for a camera. But I was just too late for a magnificent chance at a number of sailfish in the air at once, all around R. C.'s fish. It sounded, and the others did not leap again. I waited eagerly.

"Put out a bait," advised Captain Knowles.

By the time I was ready, however, R. C. had his sailfish in. He instructed the boatman to release it. So it chanced we got both our baits out together, and had strikes without even trolling. And we both hooked fish. That was the beginning of a most remarkable experience. Things happened so swiftly that I cannot recall them in sequence. But I remember some of the startling incidents. We caught those two sailfish and still the school kept passing us on each side. Sometimes a dozen or more would loom up in back of the boat, slender and sharp, swimming with fins invisible, heading south. No sooner had we put baits overboard again than we had another double-header. By the time we had whipped these two the school had passed on. It was a temptation to follow them, but, as we had many miles of Gulf Stream to travel, we could not spare the time.

I went up on top to look for more fish, and it was not long before I sighted another school. This one moved down against the stream precisely as the first one, a few leaping here and there, many breasting the current with their tails out. We maneuvered precisely as before, but could not get a strike out of this school, though we headed it, crossed from side to side, and ran on straight north through it. Not a strike! Once a sailfish approached my bait, only to refuse it.

We went on. The sun was getting high now, and about one o'clock we passed American Shoal lighthouse. It appeared a lonely place, standing on iron girders out of the sea. By and by we ran into another school of sailfish. R. C. jocularly exclaimed that this was sailfish day. He got one and I lost one out of this school. It took him quite a while to bring in a rather heavy and non-leaping fish. All the time the ripple on the sea imperceptibly darkened and deepened. Still, for the Atlantic it was a placid sea. We had expected to catch dolphin, kingfish, bonita, and cero, but nothing of the kind happened. At times we were a mile out in the Stream, though for the most part we ran right along the edge.

About two o'clock I sighted another school of sailfish, evidently more playful than the others, probably owing to the slightly ruffled water. Sailfish like rough sea. They love to ride the swells, as do Marlin swordfish.

This fourth school occupied us more than an hour, me with the camera, and R. C. on the rod. I could hardly claim that the school took that length of time in passing, but we were so long in their midst. I thought once or twice fish R. C. hooked ran with the school. Anyway, we got three sailfish out of it, two of which were lightly hooked and which we let go.

As far as the dimensions of a school of sailfish is concerned this one was the largest I ever saw. But Captain Knowles said he had seen many larger ones, one notably that took hours to pass and extended on all sides as far as he could see. There must be millions of sailfish; and always there should be splendid sailfishing. Unless some market use is discovered! Sailfish could be netted far more easily than tuna. They are, however, more difficult to locate.

We sighted something yellowish green in the water, and upon running up on it discovered two large green turtles. They astonished me by their apparent indifference to the boat. Captain Knowles explained that this was their mating season, at which time they could be easily captured. He averred that if the female was taken first the male would almost climb into the boat. Animals and fish, and birds also, exhibit a marvelous courage at such seasons.

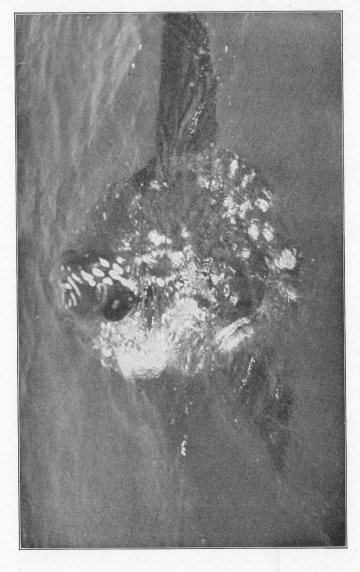

MOLA-MOLA UNDERWATER

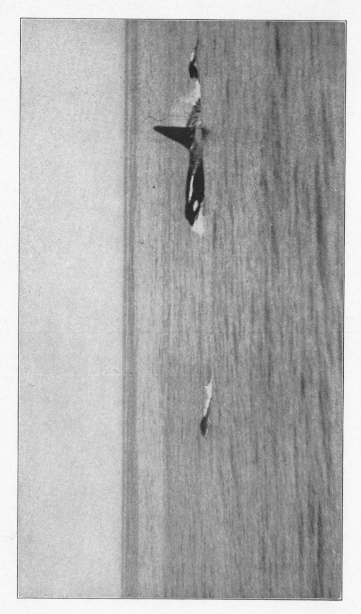

ORCA. NOTE HUGE SPIKE DORSAL FIN

I let the green turtles off with several snapshots, that I had not much hope would be good.

Not long after that I saw a large black fin cutting the water along the edge of the stream. It did not look sharp enough for a shark or notched enough for a sailfish. As we ran over I saw the fin flop over to one side, then back to the other, as did the fins of sunfish in the Pacific. But this was black, and besides I had never, in all my fishing in the Atlantic, seen a sunfish. Captain Knowles called it a *mola-mola,* which I presume is a Cuban term, and he said he had not seen a half a dozen in all his life.

We glided up to the creature, and presently I made it out to have the shape of a sunfish, but not the color I knew. This thing was a beautiful chocolate brown, spotted and streaked with white. It looked about eight feet long, almost as wide, and two feet thick through the huge blunt head. Not the least concern did it show. It was lazily rolling on the surface with huge fin flopping over from one side to the other. We circled it, ran up close, and still it padded on its way very slowly, and awkwardly, it seemed to me.

The strangeness and rarity of this marine creature strengthened my natural instinct to capture. But that was far more easily conceived than accomplished. It looked like solid bone and as if it would weigh in excess of six hundred pounds. I heartily wished for a large net into which we might tangle it. We snagged it with a heavy gang hook that held long enough for us to draw it to the surface and photograph it. When seen broadside it was indeed a beautiful and strange fish, its glazed brown hide decorated with fanciful white designs, and as big around as a dining-room table. Manifestly possessed of prodigious strength, it had no speed.   Probably it did not need either, and its long almost impenetrable hide was all the protection it required.   It had a ridiculously small mouth for so huge a fish, and I imagine was a vegetarian, if such a thing can be possible in the ocean.   It was tailless, and that half-round end of its body where the tail should have been was scalloped as gracefully as if cut by a sculptor. A fin corresponding to the huge dorsal was attached to its under side, and back of each small gill hole was a fin, round as a fan.   These kept up a continual movement, for what purpose I could not detect.   Certainly they could not have helped it swim.

Soon after our adventure with the *mola-mola* R. C. called out lustily, as if to old Neptune: "What ho! Next!"

It was interesting to wonder and conjecture about the next fish or animal or event that might confront us in this fifty-mile trolling with the current of the Gulf Stream. It was hardly probable that any other anglers had ever attempted such a fishing day.   Already we had experienced much, and the day was scarcely half over.

The combination with me as lookout and R. C. on the rod appeared to be the lucky one.   So I stuck to it, much to R. C.'s disgust.   I climbed on deck and out to the bow, where I stood in the notch of the railing.   It seemed now to be an empty sea.   The keys had vanished from sight, as had the lighthouses, and there was not even an oil-tanker blurred on the horizon.   All the more I was re-minded of the majestic and lonely Pacific.

But I did not have long to revel in this vastness and apparent emptiness, for suddenly my brother yelled.   I ran back and fell all over myself getting under the awning and down to the deck.

"Look!" cried R. C. in great excitement for him, and he pointed astern. "Son-of-gun of a Marlin! He's mad at that tarporeno teaser."

After a second or two I located the familiar purple pectoral fins standing out from each side of a good sized Marlin, like colored outriggers on a boat. What a thrill this sight gave me! But few Marlin had we ever seen in the Gulf Stream. I grasped the teaser line and jerked on it. The red-and-white plug lure described a flashing curve that appeared to excite the Marlin. He rushed it and rapped it with his bill.

"Wind in your bait," I called to R. C.

He was already doing so, and soon had the white strip of bait right alongside the Marlin. The fish saw it and sheered at it. But did not take hold!

"Oh, he's leary!" exclaimed R. C. "Tease him. We can make that fellow bite."

I jerked and hauled on the tarporeno until it executed antics calculated to enrage any reasonable fish. The Marlin appeared both curious and offended. He wagged his head with the peculiar quick motion characteristic of such fish when striking at their prey. And as I was pulling the teaser closer the Marlin came more plainly to view.

"He'll go over a hundred, R. C.," I said. "If he takes it let him have a good lot of line."

In the excitement of the moment I hardly had time to look at the Marlin, although I never lost sight of him for a moment. Still, I did not see him clearly. He was as quick as a flash. He sheered to and fro, weaved back and forth, then glided toward us to rap the teaser. He knocked it out of water. Then he dropped back a few rods, only to loom up again, colorful and beautiful. Somehow he resembled a wild species of bird underwater.

R. C. got the white ribbon of bait in front of the Marlin, between the fish and the teaser. This fact, with the remarkable maneuvers I was getting out of the tarporeno, augured hopefully for a strike.

Suddenly he rushed at both bait and teaser. At the same instant our clever boatman speeded up the engine, drawing our lures still faster through the water, and therefore more tantalizingly to the fish.

He meant business now. He sailed forward and hit at the bait—then took it. I saw the white strip curl in his mouth. R. C. yelled.

Just then the infernal tarporeno executed another lofty tumble, clear out of water. And it fell over R. C.'s line!

The Marlin sheered off and R. C.'s line caught on the teaser, making it impossible to let the fish run with the bait. We both saw disaster. But there was no remedy. The Marlin stripped the hook and vanished.

"Aw! What do you know about that?" ejaculated my brother, blankly. He sat down and gazed at me.

"Pretty tough! I'm afraid I might have prevented that —if I had pulled the tarporeno in just as he nailed your bait. But I didn't think quick enough."

I felt pretty blue about that misfortune. R. C. wanted very much to catch an Atlantic Marlin. Here was a chance at a big one—all gone!

"Well, things happen," I replied, resignedly.

"Of all the hard-luck fishermen who ever fished thirty years we are the limit," concluded my brother, and his chin bulged.

It is a favorite opinion of ours that nothing in the "fish line" ever comes easy and that only by long patience and endless endurance do we ever get results. We have had good luck at times, of course, but we have always been hard-luck fishermen. And sometimes it goes against the grain.

Whereupon once more we faced the north and the wide blue Gulf Stream, and this time with apprehensive eyes. I took the rod a while to relieve R. C. while he went up fore and had his turn at looking.

The ocean seemed dead except for moving water. Presently R. C. came aft and told us there was something showing far ahead.

"Black and shiny," he said. "Too big for porpoises."

"Orca!" exclaimed Captain Knowles, who was peering over the wheel.

That word orca brought me right about face with a jump. I gave the rod to R. C. and climbed to where I could see. Presently I discerned a black flash come up out of a white splash. It was far away. Then I saw other objects similar, though not so plain.

We steered out to head off these objects. I looked keenly, and soon was rewarded by another break of the monotonous horizon line. Whatever these things were, they did not show often.

The time came, however, when I made out the sharp, high black fin of an orca. It stood up ten feet above the sea. It was a wonderful spear-pointed organ, as thrilling a sight as that of a broadbill swordfish fin, only vastly rarer.

I went back to tell R. C. that there was a school of orca

coming. Enough said! R. C. put away the rod and, camera in hand hurried to my side.

On the moment white splashing showed, perhaps a mile distant, and then round blunt black bulks, followed by sharp fins lifting and sliding above the surface. We watched in silence while these orca showed three more times.

"What do you make out?" asked R. C.

"Five or six orca showing, one of them a buster," I replied.

"Wouldn't it just be immense if we could photograph some orca?" he queried, with hopefulness struggling to survive.

Twice before in all my experience in both seas had I seen orca; and the latter time in August, 1922, when we photographed a school of black fish or whale-killers, there was one orca we did not know was an orca until the fact came out in a photograph. That time we had run into a school of these whale-killers, somewhat akin to orca, but smaller and not so dangerous or ferocious, and found they had rounded up a school of porpoises and were devouring them. These black fish leaped for our edification, and we secured wonderful pictures. But we did not know there were orca in the bunch.

The other time I sighted orca was from the deck of the Steamship *Cabrillo* halfway between Avalon and San Pedro, also in the Pacific. There were several in this school and not until long afterward was I able to classify them. But I never forgot the round white spots on the sides of their blunt bold heads. This white spot is the distinctive mark of the orca. And orca are the most ferocious and terrible of all the wolves of the sea. They are equally dangerous to man.

As we sped out I was conscious of mingled emotions. Tense excitement and hope mingled with pessimism and doubt. How futile to attempt to photograph live orca. They were shy, wary, extremely sensitive.

But here they came, enough of them to cause R. C. and me the most intense longing. It seems hard to explain, but this sort of fishing appeals vastly to us. Added to that was the honest fear of these tigers and a grim desire to kill them. Orca kill for the sake of killing. No doubt the Creator created them, the same as the sharks, to preserve a balance in the species of the Seven Seas—to teach all the larger fish and dolphin, seals, porpoises, that the price of life was eternal vigilance. But when you know the mackerel and menhaden are gone, to make oil, and the albacore are gone, and the white sea bass are wasted for fertilizer, and that the tuna are disappearing, and that one fleet of purse-net boats caught seven million pounds of barracuda last October—without lowering the price of fish one cent per pound—and that no matter how much you would like to kill the Austrians and Japs who are robbing our seas to make a few men rich, you cannot do it,—under these circumstances it does not seem outrageous to put a grim ban on orca. At any rate, some of the scientific experts on ocean fish claim the orca should be killed.

We ran too far in front of this bunch of orca, and discovered the fact too late. They sheered somewhat toward us. When I saw the big fellow last, he was five hundred yards distant. His fin stood up like the mainmast of a schooner. How broad his back! And the motion was tremendous.

Another orca appeared far in front of the large one, and much closer to us. In fact, we were right in his path. I waited for him to come up closer. But he did not. Then I saw his color—a gleaming green-white shadow—speeding toward us. He was not so very deep. How swiftly he swam! He neared us, came into plain view not far under the surface. As he passed directly under me I saw him perfectly, a strange fish creature, long, round, black and white, with tremendous flukes. He went under the boat. I heard Captain Knowles yell something, but paid no attention at the moment. Ready to snap a picture, I waited for the others. The fact that my hands shook attested to the knowledge that I had acquired of peril on the sea. Even the veteran whale-hunters are afraid of orca.

But no more showed, and all I had for my pains was sight of some oily swirls, slicks on the surface. Nevertheless, we did not quit. We turned back on their course and went ahead full speed. When we had about given up in disappointment the orca showed again, half a mile ahead.

"Chase them," I called.

"Step on her!" yelled R. C.

And the race began. By the time the orca showed again we ascertained we would have all we could do to catch up with them. Knowles's boat could easily make ten miles an hour. We took a position somewhat seaward of them, and drove the launch to its limit. In five miles we had gained about half the distance, and during this time the orca showed at least a dozen times. There were six of them, and the huge fellow appeared like a whale in contrast.

Chasing them was about as exciting a venture as I could

THE ROUND WHITE SPOT BACK OF THE NOSE IS PLAINLY VISIBLE. THIS IDENTIFIES FISH AS AN ORCA.

ORCA, OR WHALE KILLERS, WOLVES OF THE SEA

SMALL TARPON LEAPING

imagine. Orca have been known to charge boats. Captain Knowles cites an instance near Bimini in which an orca stood by a mate that had been harpooned, and was only with great difficulty driven off. But for several rifles on board a fatality might have been recorded.

We began to snap pictures long before we got close enough to get good ones. But we were ready to take any kind of a chance.

"We're going to photograph that big orca, sure as you're born!" I shouted to R. C. And he was as thrilled as I.

They appeared to show in series, sometimes regularly and quickly for several times, then there would be a longer period before they emerged again. Sometimes the line of formation would be the same for several appearances, then again it would change. The giant orca came up between two of his mates, then to one side, and again to the other.

What a huge, sliding black hulk! And he looked his bad repute. There was nothing beautiful about him but his command over the sea. His head was bold and blunt, exceedingly sinister with its deep jaws and the strange round white spot on the side of his ugly face.

"He's tipping us the white spot," I said to R. C., thinking of the pirates and the black spot in *Treasure Island*.

"He's tipping us the chance of our lives. And don't you overlook it," responded R. C.

Then intervened one of the long periods when the orca were down. We curved a considerable distance. I felt almost sick with hope deferred. Yet we were only in pursuit of unusual pictures. Poignant feeling seemed so absurd. But I could not help it.

"Wow!" yelled R. C. And at the same instant his yell

was accompanied by a loud puff from the orca. I saw two black heads plow the water white, then shiny black backs slide into view, rise and curve, pointing the dorsal fins erect, curving the bodies, and sliding down.

"Ready! He's coming up! I see the color!" I called to R. C.

We were one hundred feet outside of that front rank. I could see many green-white glancing shapes. It was a good-sized school of orca.

The big fellow came up with a roar. His huge head showed, with its glistening white spot, then the enormous swell of his black back, and the knife-blade dorsal fin that swept in a curve high and higher. At its loftiest height I snapped my camera and yelled my exultation at the exceeding good fortune of it.

"Got him!" yelled R. C.

We raced along beside them, seeing the shadows under the surface, and were ready when they split the water. Each sight of them, especially the huge leader, seemed productive of more thrilling satisfaction. An angler can fish for sunfish, bass, and trout, or sit on the city dock and catch the homely spot or flounder, and be happy and thrilled, and just as good as any fisherman. Nevertheless, there never was a fisherman who would not have exulted in this experience. Provided, of course, he appreciated the tremendousness of it!

Under such conditions the moments sped by on wings. Before we realized it we had snapped all the films in our cameras; and then, insatiable and unreasonable, we longed for more. I dove down into the cabin and dug up another camera, with some unexposed films left. As I came out on deck Old Giant rolled over and surged and rolled out for my benefit, and I caught him squarely in the act. R. C. had no film with which to reload. But that was of small moment. The big orca did not reappear. He had been obliging enough and we would ask no more of him.

"We lost ten miles chasin' that bird," remarked R. C. "And it's three o'clock."

Soon through the haze I made out Sombrero Reef lighthouse. It was a good two hours' travel. Our houseboat was to wait for us inside of Marathon, on the reef opposite Sombrero; and in the bounds of possibility we might make our sea camp before dark.

But we ran into another school of sailfish that detained us to the extent of two fish caught, and three lost while leaping. The sun was now a magenta ball of fire, low down in the purple haze. The lights on the sea changed like those of an opal. We bade good-by to a sixty-mile run in the Gulf Stream and went in on the reef. There, in the golden shallows of coral, a dark triangular shape moving under the water attracted us. It was a giant ray, or what was locally called devil-fish. I once saw one that weighed two tons. Roosevelt took a special trip to Florida Bay to capture one of these marine animals. This one was probably ten feet across, not by any means as large as the species grow. He looked dark gray in the water. We were approaching him from behind, at perhaps fifty yards' distance, when he moved like a huge bat, apparently flying underwater. Then he leaped as slick as any leaping fish. The corners of his wings were curled. He made hardly any splash. But as he dropped back there was a loud plop, sending the spray in sheets.

R. C. looked helplessly at me

"Reckon it's just as well this day is over!"

RIVERS OF THE EVERGLADES

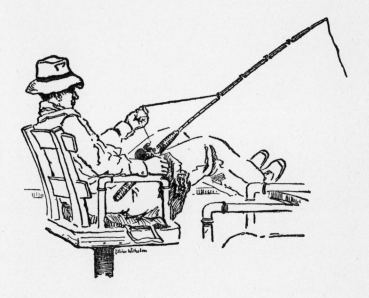

RIVERS OF THE EVERGLADES

I

Toward the end of March the gales increased in both violence and frequency, and the water grew so muddy and cold that fish were driven out to sea. As the date for my trip into the Everglades drew closer the prospect for good weather appeared more and more remote. Then, just to keep our hopes from dying, the wind shifted to the east and the temperature rose. As on many previous occasions we began to delude ourselves with a conviction that the bad weather had broken. But after a day of the prevailing trade-wind it once more veered to the south and the barometer began again to fall. It was most discouraging and exasperating. In twenty-four hours the barometer dropped to 29.70, and kept falling. The wind worked south and then southwest, a hot, moist wind. Next day almost a dead calm prevailed. Still the barometer kept falling! My boatmen, Captain Knowles and Captain Thad Williams, both native to this latitude, predicted a hard northwester. But it did not come so soon as they expected. That night and the next morning went by without any further sign of bad weather, except in that descending barometer. It dropped to 29.50. This was approaching hurricane record.

We were to board the *Ladyfish* at noon, but one thing and another kept us busy on land until late afternoon. Still, I was not so distracted by mail, telegrams, supplies, etc., that I could not keep my weather eye open. It was indeed most fascinating. There was that ominous calm! The palm trees drooped in melancholy quiet. The sea was disturbed as if by far-distant violence. To the south and west a dull black belt of cloud rolled up and moved northeast. It blotted out the westering sun. Then a warm wind sprang up again, still out of the southwest. The clouds heaved up and spread over half the sky.

About sunset a strange light, green, brilliant, shone upon the sea. I could not tell whence it came. Again the wind lulled. The cloud bank, low down, grew purple in hue. It was beautiful and fearful. Captain Williams called my attention to a rumble of thunder. It was far away. How menacing the sound! The approach of a storm is oppressive on land, but vastly more so on the sea. On the sea there is no escaping its force.

We got aboard just before the storm appeared about to break, only to find that something important had been forgotten. I went back with Captain Thad. He scanned the west and north where the black belt had lifted, showing one of gray beneath. Thunder rumbled, and lightning flashed across the darkened sky. The spray flew over the little boat, wetting me and tasting salty on my lips. It was cold. The wind struck us strong and gusty, and far across the green, tumbling, white-crested water showed the gray pall of rain.

My errand accomplished, I ran back to the dock and leaped upon the bumping launch. The rain was falling fast and cold. Darkness had about settled down, and the grim, hard sea and sky were forbidding. Yet still the storm had not broken upon us. I stood up in the rocking launch and let the rain and spray wet my face.

END OF A RUN

TARPON UPSIDE DOWN

TARPON WRESTLING TO THROW HOOK

No sooner was I safely on board the houseboat than the northwester struck us with heavy wind and rain. Darkness fell, and the roar of sea and gale was something to arouse fear in one who respected the elements. I watched for the flashes of lightning, and when they came I saw the angry lashing sea and the deluge of rain and the scudding black clouds, in a most wonderful fleeting instant.

Everyone at Long Key had advised against our undertaking the trip in the face of past bad weather, with worse impending. R. C. did not show any rapture over the prospect. But I found myself on board because I did not particularly hate storms and because I always believed the sun would shine to-morrow or next day, or some day. I am a sun worshiper, like a desert Indian or an Arab, yet I fancy I could not appreciate it or love it so much if I had never the contrast of leaden sky and stinging sleet or freezing rain. Anyway, we were on board, comfortable in the spacious brightly lighted salon of the houseboat, and the deluge was roaring on the roof, and the waves pounding on the hull. By and by the fury of the storm abated and only a pattering of rain drops or a gust of wind made us aware of the inclement weather outside. During the night I heard the wind moaning round the boat and felt the slow heave of the sea. Morning dawned bright and steely, with a northwester in full blast. Nevertheless, we weighed anchor and bit into the teeth of it. If this book were to be a chronicle of bad weather I might have much material. But bad weather is only something to make us love good weather. Every storm cloud had golden sunshine at the back of it.

March 27th was a beautiful summer day, and East Cape

Sable was a lonely green-fringed white-beached shore that invited exploration. We anchored just off the most easterly point of Cape Sable. The beach curved in a league-long line from this point to the next; a gleaming half circle under the sun, lapped by rippling green waves, and bordered by cocoanut palms, at this season with green and gold drooping leaves and gray slanting trunks. The grove on the point was open, sunny, colorful, full of soft rustlings of leaves, and fragrantly dry.

Lines of exquisite shells, left by each tide, and therefore always changing, made the beach glistening white and rose and pink and pearl gray, so delicate and beautiful that it seemed sacrilege to walk crushingly over the fragile mounds and lines. It was indeed a shore of shells; and the white-and-gold sand consisted of sea shells broken to atoms by the waves.

If there is anything I love it is to wander along a lonely shore. I was not able to wander far, or gather many shells, or invite my dreams under the shady palms, out of the blinding glare and heat, because brother R. C. espied tarpon rolling. He always complains to people of the strenuous life I lead him, from one hard place to another, but I have observed that in cases like this he sees the fish first.

Indeed, tarpon were rolling in shore and off shore. The water was not quite clear, being a greenish-yellow color, more like river water than that of the sea. Perhaps the rivers of fresh water pouring from the vast Everglades have some little effect in this coloration. The tarpon had come in from the sea, through the green channels, on their way up these rivers.

The rolling of tarpon had always been fascinating to

me. I first saw it in the Panuco River at Tampico, Mexico. It is merely a fish habit, like any other, and consists of a lazy roll to the surface, showing sometimes the whole body. According to the light the color of tarpon varies. Here one would look green-backed, there tinged by gold or bronze, and again all silvery. When a tarpon showed in the sun he shone like a burnished shield.

Wherefore R. C. and I went trolling in Captain Thad's small launch. With the easy motion, the comfortable seats, the green foliage of the shore line, and the rolling of tarpon, it was more than delightful. R. C.'s terse remark was pertinent:

"Well, if you'd ask me, I'd say with fish striking this would be some sport!"

These tarpon did not appear to be striking. But the pleasure of riding among them on that rippling water close to the white beach was all-satisfying. By and by, however, I had a tarpon strike. My hook appeared to have attached itself to a log. I knew, though, that the obstruction was alive—a tarpon. It was the feel of it. We were using light tackle and I struck as hard as I dared.

"Ha! You've hung one!" called R. C.

The water exploded and out came the fish, a small one, about fifty pounds, and he shook himself so swiftly that he blurred in my sight. That was why it was so difficult to obtain clearly defined pictures of leaping tarpon. This fellow cracked down, popped up again, and wrestled in the air, turning over. After that he danced out and back and around, affording R. C. some fun, but little chance for good pictures. Still he took what he offered.

When I brought the tarpon to the boat Captain Thad lifted it half out and, carefully extricating the hook, released it. This appeared to be the only method pertaining to such tarpon fishing and if sharks are not present the released fish may live.

We saw several good-sized tarpon roll, and hoped to hook one of these. In the next hour R. C. caught two, one about sixty-five pounds, the other forty, out of which we got some pretty leaps. At sunset the tarpon ceased rolling and we returned to the boat.

I lingered out on deck to watch this sunset. The west had a purple band of cloud that stretched long thin lines across the face of the sun. It gave a bizarre effect. The hue of the sun was a golden crimson, not too intense for the gaze to bear. Gradually the shades all deepened. The sun began to grow oblong, like an exquisite Japanese vase; and then came the moment, the optical illusion, when it seemed to elongate, to reach down and suck up the sea. It sank very quickly, the last edge of curved fire slipping out of sight with a strange impressiveness. Then the short twilight fell.

II

MIDDLE CAPE had all the attractive features of East Cape, and in addition a magnificent grove of larger cocoanut palms, and a level point of white sand that extended some way out into the sea. As we passed by I saw a flock of terns sitting on the sand, heads all pointing to the wind.

Beyond Middle Cape the topography of the beach took a radical change and features more in harmony with the word sable began to be manifest. No more graceful palms! A dark-green line of brush and sedge absorbed the narrowing sandy beach. North West Cape stood out boldly. Once round that I could see the great wall of mangrove forest, grim and forbidding, facing the Gulf defiantly. The Everglades hid behind this barrier, far in the interior. My gaze took in leagues of mangrove wall, of an irregularity beyond description, a lofty front of solid green, striped by myriads of tree trunks. Many were dead and bleached white. All along, this wall showed the effect of wind and sea battering at this protective forest, at the stubborn obstacle nature had thrown up against the encroachments of the Gulf. In some places the sea builds up; in others it seeks to destroy. This was the windward side of the fortification of the Everglades, and it showed the ravages and scars.

Rivers of the Everglades, large and small, broke the hard green phalanx, where they emptied their dark waters into the Gulf.

Mystery hovered over this forbidden place, neither land nor water nor forest, yet a combination of all three. Though the sun shone brightly and the sky was azure and the breeze breathed off a summer sea, this wilderness of waterways and endless ramifications of mangrove forest did not invite with the bright face of nature, did not beckon to the adventuring soul. It repelled. It boded ill. It was of the salt, hard, caustic, bitter. Never before had I seen a forest that did not lure. But this was not a forest; it was a sinister growth out of the coral.

We anchored off one of the mouths of the Shark River, far enough out in the bay to catch the breeze. The tide was on the ebb. Captain Thad bundled us into the small boat, with tackle, bait, cameras, and in half an hour steered us into the mouth of a creek invisible until we were right upon it.

We were about to penetrate the mangrove forest. Here the impressions were different, more intimate, less menacing, and, owing to the undefiled shore line, they took on some semblance of beauty.

The mangroves bore glistening leaves; the branches and trunks were gray, yellow, almost red; the roots formed a marvelous matted network out of which the tree trunks rose. Three feet of black mud full of crab holes stood between the water line and the level. A light-green lacy moss, almost like ferns, covered the edge of the banks and drooped over. Gleams of sunshine penetrated the thick foliage. Shadow and light, color and movement abided between those gnarled roots and the canopy of leaves, and what in another forest made for beauty and charm here attracted by a strange character, steely and flinty. Yet a certain kind of lure began to dawn on me. This was a country that must be understood. Blue herons, white cranes, snipe, and unknown birds fled silently at our approach. In places the spreading branches leaned gracefully to the water. Shaded channels, dim and mysterious, opened into the forest; and always a lonely water fowl was in evidence.

At length we came to where this passageway entered a larger creek, something over a hundred feet wide. A breeze ruffled the water; the tips of the mangroves waved and threshed. The widening circles and foam globules on the smooth surface of the amber water attested to the presence of tarpon. We ran the bow of the launch into the mud of the bank and prepared to fish.

Now to troll for tarpon in open rivers or swift channels or shallow bays adjacent to the sea is one kind of fishing; this was decidedly another. No greater contrast could be found in angling for the same species of fish.

The kind we were soon adopting had more to recommend it, perhaps, than the other. We were in the lonely forest wilderness, strange despite the sunlight, silent somehow, for all the cry of birds. No sooner had I my bait out than I began to try to grasp this singular charm. First, I was fishing. That fact was the great shibboleth. We were located in a lonely nook, far from the haunts of men. The grim forest inclosed us, insulating us, barring us from the open. It was a different kind of wildness. Mangroves were born of salt. They nourished their hideous powerful roots, like knots of snakes, in salt water. Cranes and herons, as silent as this home of theirs, winged lumbering flight to and fro. By and by the wind died down, and then there was a deep silence, broken at intervals by bird notes. Once a giant woodpecker pounded on a dead mangrove, and the sound was like an electric hammer. Once I heard the song of a redbird, but his song was melancholy, as if he regretted resting there on his way north.

And up and down the gleaming, shadowy creek tarpon were rolling. Here in this quiet water they slipped out, nose and fin and tail, seldom making more than a ripple and some patches of foam. Sometimes a large one churned the water in his swirl. Another would make a noise almost like a puff. They were there in abundance, large and small, showing in a creek they could almost leap across. That was the unbelievable and thrilling fact to me. Hundred-pound tarpon in a creek no larger than the sunfish brooks of my youth! Then to see them and hear them added wonderfully to the excitement. Far down the creek

I would get a glimpse of a dark feathery fin disappearing; nearer at hand I would espy a swirl on the water and tell-tale bubbles; right over my line a big silver fish lazily broke the mirroring surface; and behind me, upstream, I heard the gentle souse of a rolling tarpon. All this while I was holding my line in sensitive fingers, waiting for a bite. But none came. R. C. was as engrossed as I. To see and hear all these tarpon so close by was a new and remarkable experience. I really did not expect to get a bite. I had been used to having tarpon almost jerk me overboard on their strike. But here we were assured they bit very gently—just a tug and slow movement away.

The color of these giant herring of the sea appealed to me most of all. In that subdued light they had backs of pearl gray and sides of silvery pink, almost rose. They shone with soft iridescence. As long as they so obligingly rolled on the surface in plain sight just so long did they make their beauty mine. It is a great privilege to have a fish, a denizen of the mysterious depths, rise to the light for your edification and profit.

Time sped by. The sun sank; the breeze died; the tarpon ceased to roll; the vast gloom of an unknown region seemed to settle down. And clouds of gnats, almost too tiny to see, and small black mosquitoes, made the last half hour almost unendurable. Finally we gave up and raced down the labyrinthine channel toward the sea. What relief the breeze that freed us from our tormentors!

III

At six o'clock in the morning a soft pink glow suffused the east. Though it was clear daylight, the air appeared

LIKE A SPECTER OF A FISH

TARPON, OR SILVER KING

full of mist and the dark lines of mangrove forest were dim and mystical. A cool, fresh, balmy damp breeze came from off the water. Drops of dew dripped like rain from the upper deck of the boat; the lower deck was wet; everything showed the presence of moisture.

The sun rose a dull red through the thin fog, and gained in brightness until it was gold fire. A track of gold crossed the waters.

At seven o'clock we were on the little launch, dragging rowboats and speeding for the mangroves. By the time we had reached the mouth of the river where we had entered yesterday the sun was shining hot and a warm wind was ruffling the bay.

The tide appeared to be on the rise and about halfway in. We were somewhat late, as Captain Thad likes best to start in with a rising tide. Moreover, the water in the river was muddy from the incoming flow. Entering the creek from the river, we were soon in the cool shade of the spreading mangrove branches. White cranes and blue herons rose to fly before our advance. In and around the meandering water course we glided on, and before eight o'clock reached the wider place where we had seen the rolling tarpon. Not one was visible this morning.

Captain Thad did not particularly like the tide and conditions, but decided to try fishing, anyway; and soon R. C. and Knowles had lines out from the opposite bank, and we did likewise from our side. Then we settled down to wait.

The morning was pleasant, and I began to make the most of it Presently I heard the soft surge of a rolling tarpon. That was music to expectant ears. Captain Thad said he saw a big one break water down the creek. Soon

I spied a big transparent fin splitting the water upstream. No more was needed to make the waiting period one of keen anticipation.

More music of birds was in evidence this morning—the whistle of redbird, kingfisher, osprey, the caw of a crow, and piercing note of the woodpecker. At least two unfamiliar bird notes rang on the air.

A tarpon surged not fifteen feet from where R. C. sat in the skiff. Next, one broke near the boat where I waited, and another rolled just over my line. How tantalizing the blaze of silver! Several more rolled within sight, and then followed the usual spell of blank water. Under such circumstances time passed fleetly. The tide was running in almost at flood when a sharp whistle from R. C. electrified us.

As I looked I wondered how many thousands of times in my life I had shot an eager gaze across a space of water to see if my brother had a bite. He was standing up, rod extended, in an attitude that never failed to thrill me. I saw his line running out, upstream, not far from the opposite bank.

"Look sharp!" called R. C. "I'm going to soak him!"

He swept up the light rod and it bent double. The line strung straight, lifted by a moving weight. Then I saw a deep furrow in the water.

"Ready! He's coming up," yelled R. C.

A heavy splash preceded the wagging shape of a tarpon. He came half out, crashing the water white. I snapped the camera on him. He plunged down and, making a wide turn, headed away from us. In another moment we judged from his manner of action that he was not much of a leaper. Nevertheless, as R. C. tried to hold him, finding it impossible on the nine-thread line, he made a sousing splash, out of which he stood three-quarters of his length.

"Hundred pounder!" yelled R. C.

"Yes, and you've got light tackle!" I yelled back. "Hold him just hard enough to make him jump."

During the following few moments the tarpon broke water several times, affording me opportunities for pictures. But he did not perform such acrobatics as we were looking for. And at length he settled down under the surface and gave R. C. all he wanted to risk on the light tackle, without rowing after him to recover line. Once he was round the bend downstream out of R. C.'s sight. Again he crossed the creek and swam upstream close to the bank, under the leaning mangroves. R. C. was hard put to it to drag him from butting into the launch. He went two hundred yards upstream before he tired of that. On his way back R. C. got the line in and hung to it doggedly. The finish of the fight ranged within fifty feet of the skiff. He took a good deal of handling, and whenever he was brought near the skiff he threshed and pounded, splashing boatman and angler, to our great enjoyment. They had a most difficult time with him, or at least Captain Knowles had, for on the several instances when he grasped the leader he was deluged. Once he disappeared behind flying water and spray. But finally he secured the tarpon with a stout rope and detached the hook.

"Hundred an' fifteen pounds, I'd say," called Knowles.

"Well," sang out my brother, and I knew what he was going to say, "I'm ahead of you. Better get a move on."

We fished for another hour, without seeing a tarpon roll or getting a strike. At flood tide the water was too muddy. No doubt the fish had gone up the channel into the clearer creeks that bisected the mangroves. We gave up for the day, more than satisfied.

When we reached the mouth of the river and turned into the bay we ran into a hard southeast wind and a choppy sea that wet us thoroughly by the time we reached the houseboat.

In Florida waters tarpon are caught by trolling, drifting, and still fishing. Crabs and mullet are the best baits. Small tarpon will strike at a spoon when they are in playful mood. Trolling, of course, is the most strenuous and sportsmanslike method of the three. In deep water a strike from a heavy tarpon is a violent shock and something to remember. Moreover, added to the thrill of the tremendous strike there are the swift runs and lofty tumbles peculiar to this fish when hooked. His endurance, too, is tenfold what it appears to be in shallow water. I have had some memorable fights with tarpon, upward of three hours and more, and in only one of these battles did I finally conquer the fish. For such large tarpon light tackle would not be my choice. But on the shoals of the Everglades and at the mouths of the rivers and in the small creeks more sport and excitement are to be had with the light rigs.

At flood tide the following day Captain Thad guided our houseboat, dragging its launches and skiffs, into the green winding lane that was called Shark River. The name was a misnomer. In the first place, there were no sharks. In the second place, it was a winding green creek, with many side channels, making the mangrove forest a matter of many islands. Some were large, but most were small and round or oval, with dark-green foliage rising to a graceful mound. The heavy timber extended for miles.

NESTS AND EGGS OF CURLEW

CURLEW FRIGHTENED FROM NESTS

A CREEK AT THE HEAD OF SHARK RIVER

R. C. HOOKED TO ANOTHER TARPON

But at length the forests gave place to mangrove shrubbery, broken at intervals, where the level grassy plain of the Everglades gave welcome to the seeking eyes.

Twenty miles or more from the sea we dropped anchor in a wide island-dotted lake of amber-colored river water. Birds were sailing about; small fish were rippling the surface.

From here we departed in the launch to take one of the many estuaries running into the lake. Its many turns were bewildering and its tributaries or branches were innumerable. We glided down shaded lanes where we had to bend our heads to escape the low-spreading branches. Deep creeks of amber water, with banks of heavy foliage, where ducks and cranes and herons rose, and fish splashed on the surface, appealed particularly to me. We saw numerous alligators as they came sliding off the banks. In and out and around we went, through this labyrinthine web of waterways, at last to emerge into a beautiful long stretch of stream, quite wide, where the brown water was glinting with flash of silver tarpon and wild fowl seemed thick as bees.

We trolled up this long green-bordered lane, catching some of the baby tarpon on bass tackle, and also several snook, a game fish about which we had heard much. He looked something like a pickerel, was a silvery yellow underneath, gray-green on the back, and had a black stripe down the median line. Those we caught were small, but they struck hard, fought well, and leaped repeatedly.

Soon we began to see the flocks of birds, like white clouds, rising from the trees, and knew we were nearing the wonderful rookery of curlew. So we put away our rods for our cameras.

Though we saw birds everywhere, in the air and on the foliage, we were not in the least prepared for what a bend in the stream disclosed. Banks of foliage as white with curlew as if with heavy snow! With tremendous flapping of wings that merged into a roar, thousands of curlew took wing, out over the water. They flew across the stream, soaring high, and, circling, they sailed round back of us, to swoop down. For half a mile, as we passed up the creek, this flight and noise of birds was incessant. It was a most wonderful experience.

Once, at the point where the rookery was most thickly populated, Captain Thad yelled at the top of his lungs. Then rose a deafening din. Thousands of curlew on their nests took wing, crashing up out of the foliage, and, joining the thousands of male birds, they darkened the light of the sun.

R. C. and I had Captain Thad set us ashore, which was accomplished easily, and he left us there. We found solid ground and a thorny jungle, the whole of which appeared splotched white with guano. Nests were everywhere, close to the ground and up over our heads, so many that they touched one another. Most of them contained two green-speckled, rather brownish eggs; some had three; a few of them had one. These nests were built of sticks and appeared to have been used for years.

We separated, with the idea of lying low till the curlew returned. To that end I sat down under a shady mangrove. R. C. stole off some distance and disappeared.

The sky above me appeared streaked with the white birds. A low roar of wings kept up continually. At once I observed that only in my immediate vicinity had the curlew left their nests, and those that had vacated were coming back by hundreds. The tips of the trees bent with the weight of alighting birds. They were really very tame. In a few moments curlew were all around me and above me, and the nests, except those only a few feet from me, were again occupied. The roar of wings died down. When it ceased a strange crooning sound persisted. This was made by the curlew, but whether it was a song or an uneasy utterance, I could not tell. Very gradually it died away.

I sat there for an hour, until perfect peace had returned to the rookery. Birds were as thick as the leaves. Indeed, white prevailed over green. Those curlew near enough to see me kept wary watch. But for the most part their haunt might not have been invaded by man. I had no way to estimate their number. Half a mile of the stream bank, a hundred yards deep into the jungle, was a white mass of nesting and resting curlew!

So much of beauty and birdlife, so wild that it was tame, seemed a rare and marvelous fact of nature. The great spirit of creation was brooding here.

Presently I set about trying to get pictures, which, despite unexampled opportunities, I did not succeed in accomplishing to my satisfaction. Perhaps I took too much caution not to scare the curlew. And as they did not appear greatly to fear me, I selected a lofty tree, easy to climb, and soon sat astride a comfortable perch on the level with the tree crests. There had been much excitement among the curlew during my climb. From nearby they rose in flapping clouds, circled and soared and sailed. The strange crooning, moaning sound once more rose. As best I could I began to snap pictures. It was not so easy as it had appeared from below. Reloading my camera, I settled down, motionless, to wait for exceptional pictures.

Precisely as before, the curlew soon returned to the trees near where I sat, and gradually quieted down. The hens worked back to their nests, and the males sat in white rows on every branch of every treetop I could see. By actual count there were twenty-three nests in the treetop I had chosen for my outlook. Only the nests farthest away from my perch were again visited by the owners. But in all the trees adjacent the curlew went back to setting. Birds alighted in my tree, a dozen feet from me, and when I moved to focus the camera on them they flew. I had to be content with photographing them a little farther away. Then when my second and last roll of film was finished I had, of course, wonderful opportunities. Curlew stood on the topmost branch, nine in a row, peering at me. They were really beautiful birds, long necked, long legged, and long billed, white as snow except for the tips of their wings, which were black, and in size they equalled a young turkey. Their yellow bills were long, and manifestly developed to dig in the mud for whatever they subsisted on.

After a time I noted a different species of bird, much the same in size and build, but of a decided soft pinkish color. It had a longer and more striking bill. This bird I recognized as the roseate spoonbill. Careful survey of the surrounding treetops discovered only a few of this kind. I clung to my perch until I was so weary and aching that I thought I would fall out. Yet I was reluctant to abandon it. I felt like Peter Pan who lived in the treetops. To be sure, all the treetops in fairyland were similar to these. I certainly wished for my youngsters, especially Loren, who loves birds and does not yet seem to have developed the killing instinct common to boys.

R. C. called from somewhere below, and an uproar ensued.   The curlew above where he stood began to take noisy flight.   Then Captain Thad's launch came back up the stream.   I found myself amidst a roar and a white cloud and a most singularly vivid maelstrom of rising, flapping, flying, and sailing birds.   A sea of moving white reached across the green jungle.

Upon reaching the ground I found my hands and clothes thick with dirt from these bird-infested trees.   We clambered aboard the launch and left the bank amid a flapping, moaning din.   As we started away I busied myself for a few moments brushing off my clothes.   Upon glancing up and back again I was thrilled by the most beautiful sight of the day, and perhaps of all bird sights in my experience.

Myriads of curlew were swooping back down the river, sailing with wide wings spread, and the setting sun was shining fairly upon them.   They sailed down and forward in a continuous stream, level and close, with not one single pair of wings flapping.   It was an exquisitely strange and colorful action.   Almost a waterfall of white birds!   When the foremost ranks reached the green bank of their rookery they seemed to crowd together in a white mass, like frothy water at the foot of a rapid.   Then my gaze went back to the sailing stream.   How pure and white in the sunlight! They were as graceful as swans.   And the multitude, the ever-sailing, endless ranks of curlew, reaching from the dark water far up into the sky, silhouetted first against green and then against blue, kept gliding down in wondrous flight until a bend of the river intervened to hide them.

Next morning we left the bay by a different water route,

to the north and west, and traversed meandering creeks for into the Everglades.

It was hot summer weather, even though the date said March. No sea breeze penetrated to these inland waters. The air was drowsy, still, humid. In a shady narrow creek where the current glided perceptibly and the water looked deep we took to the skiff and, rowing along under the lee of one shelving bank of green, we cast for black bass. They did not run large and were of the big-mouthed variety, yet they afforded welcome change and sport. Besides, fresh water fish for the table was something new.

First we used spinners, and then a hideous red contraption with spinner and pork rind, both of which were quite fetching, especially the latter. R. C. was casting with a small light bait rod, and I was using a fly rod. He handled the situation better than I, and very cheerfully acquainted me with the fact. Presently he hung his spinner over a mangrove branch and, pulling hard, broke his leader, which fact was productive of language.

Wild fowl were continually flying by and over us, some swooping up in alarm, others indifferent to our presence. I heard the squawk of crane or heron. Presently it occurred to me that I had in my box one of the Wilder-Dilg black-bass flies which bore my name. The genial inventors of these flies had assured me that all of them were wonderful, and particularly the one named after me. Now it chanced that I knew these gentlemen had made precisely the same claim to several other anglers who, like me, had been honored by having flies named after them. It was very nice of Wilder and Dilg to flatter us that way, but I thought it a little fishy. Anyway, I had never tried the

Zane Grey bug, and here was my opportunity. So I put
it on.

With immense doubt and something of thrill and a
smattering of conscious pride, I made an elaborate cast.
For the first time that day I cast where I had aimed. This
was a shady nook with golden depths where a little eddy
swirled. As the fly lit on the water there came a flash, a
boil, and a plop. Something heavy went down and appro-
priated my treasured fly for himself, also part of my leader.

"Big snook!" exclaimed R. C., who had watched with
interest. "Gimme one of those Z. G. bugs."

"It was the only one I had," I replied, in distress.

"Say, if I had a great fly like that named after me, I'd
pack a lot of them around," said R. C.

"Well, I'll name a steam winch after you some of these
days," I retaliated. My boatman at Avalon and I used
to apply this sobriquet to R. C. when he was hauling away
on a swordfish. It was very felicitous.

When we quit fishing for black bass, which was owing
to a sense of guilt at catching so many, we turned back
on the long way to the launch. Presently Captain Thad
took a side channel, where we had to push through the
foliage. It opened another of the tortuous lanes. But
there was a difference in this one, in that the water was
dead, like that of a pond. It was full of grass and moss
and weed, likewise many fish, the only one of which I
could name was a gar.

This lane of slack water ended in a wide basin that
opened right into the Everglades. By using the skiff we
crossed it, at last to get out and stand on that mysterious
land called the glades. The grass in places was higher
than my head. With some effort I wormed myself into the

forks of a sapling on the bank, and was enabled to see out over the Everglades.

It was a prairie, dotted by patches of trees, and in these I recognized what are named hammocks. They were round and dense, apparently growing on more elevated or at least solid ground. The color was green with a tinge of yellow. Far as eye could see stretched this wasteland, this desert of grass and sedge and isolated trees. Wild fowl crossed my vision, near and far, lending color and life to the scene. Heat veils were rising, thin, transparent, yet somehow like smoke.

If I had been able to get high enough to see over that wilderness I felt the sight would have been vastly impressive. As it was I had to be content with a glimpse of the lonely glades.

When I returned to the skiff, R. C. and the men were catching little alligators. I was to hear my first baby alligator grunting most vociferously for its parent. Interesting as this sound was, and the mystery of the hidden nook whence the sound came, I was using most of my faculties to avoid meeting the youngster's mother, that Captain Thad assured us was near. Having had an education relative to alligators and crocodiles in Mexico, I repaired to the skiff, from which I watched my brother wading around in the muck, quite full of boyish glee.

This place was a shallow end of one of the blind waterways and it appeared to be a paradise for birds and reptiles. The water was hot. Everywhere it was ridged by moving creatures under the surface, in the slimy moss. Presently I was highly delighted by locating several small alligators with their snouts out of the water. They were watching me, apparently as interested in me as I was in

them. Dragon flies and water snakes reminded me of the
ponds of my boyhood fishing days. There was a spell
here, of the sun and the open, of water and rushes, of
things that moved yet could not be seen, of wild birds and
solitude. My one sense most powerfully affected was that
of smell—something I did not discover at first.

A hot, moist, dank odor breathed off the stagnant water,
and the gentle breeze coming from the Everglades hinted
of many such spots as this. And all at once the peculiar
odor carried me back to the weedy ponds of my youth, to
bullfrog chasing days, and fearful quests for snapping
mud turtles, and to the golden summers, hot, drowsy,
sweet, so long ago and far away.

IV

WE spent another day at anchor in this inland bay, and
then traveled with the outgoing tide down toward the sea.
A channel led from Shark River into Harney River, and
we traversed that, winding among islands, through narrow
swift channels, at last out into the open water.

Harney River had many mouths, some of them mere
leafy lanes leading from the mangroves to the sea. All
along the front of the forest here were oyster beds, shallow
reefs with passages cut by the tides. Perhaps owing to
these reefs, which protected the mangroves, there was
here no high grim scarred wall of trees, but a series of
billowy green islands standing on the mangrove stilts.
The groves and islets and bowers were enchanting to the
eye, if one forgot about the hard nature of the mangroves
and salt water.

Next morning we were off at seven o'clock, with all

conditions favorable. This time Captain Thad took us up a good-sized river to a pond where it forked. Tarpon were rolling and working up the left fork, but we did not see one show in the other branch. R. C. went across the river at the mouth of this left fork, and fished out from there. We tied up to the shore directly opposite. Now and then I heard the souse and "poff" of a rolling tarpon. They were working up on R. C.'s side.

The morning was hot and still—a very delightful opportunity for sandflies and mosquitoes, which they made the most of. I fought them with one hand while I held my rod with the other. Under the circumstances it would have been difficult then to substantiate arguments as to the good time I was having. Some things are hard to explain. Fishing is a condition of mind wherein you cannot possibly have a bad time.

Almost at the start we heard R. C.'s warning whistle. All of us went through excitement and action, getting ready for a tarpon to show. This fish, however, was a shark. When we were all settled again to watch and wait, R. C. had a real strike. I saw his line fly out and a furrowed bulge on the water.

A sodden thumping splash followed, and I caught a good-sized tarpon halfway out. He sounded, made a lunge, and broke water again, coming out about the same as on the first break. I snapped this bit of action. Then, to my chagrin, the tarpon leaped swiftly, clear out, in a beautiful curve, wrestling so convulsively that we plainly heard him. He plunged out of sight. I wound my camera to another film. But he did not show again.

For half an hour I stood, camera in hand, waiting patiently for the fish to leap. He was a dogged fighter

and gave R. C. all he could do to handle him without following him in the skiff.   Sometimes he was two hundred
yards down the river, and at others far up the branch.   In
one of his circles he came within thirty feet of us, swirling
on the surface.   R. C. eventually wore him out and brought
him to Captain Knowles's eager hands.

"About hundred and thirty," called out Knowles.
"We're pickin' a heavier one every day."

Two hours more brought no further results, and at
length the tarpon ceased to roll or passed on out of sight.
We went back to the houseboat.

I was glad of the fact that Knowles could make good
use of all the tarpon we were likely to catch.   He dressed
them and cut out choice portions, which he salted thoroughly and laid in the sun to dry.   Knowles had been born
and brought up among the conch fishermen and sponge
fishermen of Key West, and he said they had taught him
not to waste fish.

This is one reason why I think Key West will some
day be renowned as a fishing resort.   Another reason is
that the fish are there in great numbers.   Charles Frederick
Holder wrote his best book, *The Log of a Sea Angler,*
about water adjacent to Key West.   The Dry Tortugas,
islands some sixty miles distant, and too far for the market
fishermen, offer opportunities to anglers who can stand
hardships.

The next morning was warm, still, cloudy, dark, somehow threatening.   How gloomy the long capes of mangroves!   Impenetrable and inscrutable they seemed.   In
spite of the glamour of fishing and the lure of the open,
this mangrove barrier and the glades beyond had fastened
their repellant spell upon my mind.   I began to reflect upon

what strange and terrible effect this environment must have on living creatures, especially human beings.

The Everglades harbored the remnant of a remarkable race of Indians—the Seminoles—and several isolated settlements of fishermen and many outcasts, plume-hunters, and bootleggers.

We went fishing, as usual, expecting a more favorable day and better tides and clearer water. A fisherman should hope always, yet expect nothing for that particular occasion. Our favorite creek ·was muddy; the larger stream appeared deserted by tarpon; another place we found, a broad inland bay surrounded by islands, was full of tarpon that would not bite.

The hours dragged by. It was one of those occasions when I had to discover something new or else call it a profitless day. Nature is so manifold in its works and so incessant in its life that there is hardly a conceivable place where the senses of man cannot be beguiled.

Opportunity afforded to watch an Everglade kite, a rare bird I had not seen before. This one soared above us, round and round, swooping down to the treetops. It was about the size of a pigeon, only more slender, a little longer, and it possessed a remarkable build. It was a giant swallow. The wings were perfectly bowed, without the abrupt bend as in eagles, hawks, and other birds of prey. The tail was wide with a very deep fork. Its head appeared small. Perhaps its most striking feature was the color. The under side of the wings was half black, half white, and the tail had the same beautiful markings. The black margin was on the outside. Captain Thad said the back of this bird was blue, and also that it lived on insects. Some of its swift flights downward lent credence to this state-

ment. Twice I saw it swoop down to a dead branch and
strike at something there, or grasp it with swift bill. In
beauty, grace, and wildness this Everglade kite equaled
the frigate-bird of the keys.

Next I heard an owl. In broad daylight, in such a place,
this sound seemed incredible. But it was a fact Captain
Thad averred was common. So I listened. Again I heard
it, and yet again. Woo, hoo-hoo woooo hoo! Its melancholy and dismal refrain seemed heightened by the inhospitable mangrove forest.

About that time I had a bite. Something tugged at my
line. Pesky little catfish! I paid no heed. Suddenly the
line slid out swiftly, and before I could get into a position
to strike a fair-sized tarpon leaped, throwing the bait ten
feet. R. C. saw this from his skiff below, and he called
out, tantalizingly, "April fool!" Thus I was reminded
of the date.

Two o'clock came and passed. The heat was thick and
heavy, despite a clouded sky. Mosquitoes hummed. Birds
and tarpon apparently had abandoned such luckless anglers
as we were.

Suddenly something bit me fiercely through my shirt. I
cried out, dropped my rod, and frantically slapped at my
shoulder where the hot sting appeared to be. A huge
black fly dropped to the floor of the launch. It was crushed,
yet still alive.

"Horsefly," said Captain Thad, casually. "He's only a
little one. Wait till a big one bites you."

"Humph! This fellow did quite well," I replied. He
had brought the blood, and the bite burned acutely, so I
was constrained to acquire information about this dis-
turber of my peace. He resembled the common horsefly

I had observed in the forests and deserts of the West, yet he appeared more vividly colored. Captain Thad said the Everglades was infested by this fly and that it increased in numbers as warm weather advanced. It was a honey-sucker like a bee, living mostly on the palmetto blossoms, and also on the black mangrove flowers. Naturally, it was a blood-sucker, too. Captain Thad said his father had once tried to keep a small herd of cattle near Fort Myers.

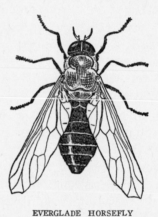

EVERGLADE HORSEFLY

He lives on honey from blossoms, but when occasion offers he will bite a man

It was absolutely necessary to keep the cattle corralled during the daylight, with smudge fires burning all the time. Only at night could the animals graze. He related also of business men stocking a range on the Everglades with a big herd of cattle. The horseflies killed most of the stock, and drove the rest so far away they were never found. Captain Knowles told about a pig jumping over-board from his boat because of the bite of one of these flies.

At dawn we left Harney River and, making a wide detour to avoid shoals, we went up the coast line to anchor at the mouth of Broad River. The low broken forest line and the many islands gave this locality a different aspect, pleasing where the last had been forbidding. The sun rose bright gold. The wind had returned to the northeast, the best quarter for our comfort and success, and the air was cool, fresh, pleasant, without the humid, enervating quality of the last few days.

Captain Thad's man, Bob King, an expert fisherman of the West Coast, had joined us with his boats, and he reported tarpon running thick in the channels entering Broad River. We were soon off with launches and skiffs. This day promised to be very pleasant. An off-shore breeze rippled the water, which had begun to clear.

Nearing the mouth of Broad River, we ran in among beautiful islands, from one single mangrove bush to a clump of mangrove trees rising on their writhing, distorted roots. These islands strung across the shoals outside of where the many channels of Broad River entered the sea. They changed the grim aspect of the coast line. On the inside of these islands we found shoals and channels and little bays where tarpon were rolling. We ran the boats up on bars and hurried preparations for fishing. The tide had just started to come in and tarpon were lolling and rolling about, waiting for the rise of water. Mosquitoes and sandflies were notable for their absence, a most welcome circumstance. White cranes and blue herons were stalking along the bars, feeding, or standing motionless to watch us. Porpoises were making the water fly into sheets as they pursued mullet and catfish over the shoals. I saw one porpoise shoot through the water, leaving great furrows,

and go half his length out on the mudbar. How he wiggled
and flopped to get back! Pelicans were soaring and swooping, intent upon their morning meal. Flocks of wild ducks
dotted the shining surface of the bay. Songs of birds
came faintly from the distant mangroves. And all around
our position could be heard the souse and splash and "poff"
and surge of rising tarpon. Some of them broke water
within fifteen feet of us. Along the edge of the bars
waving glassy fins and green backs could be seen. Then
came a splashing roar on the surface where a tarpon had
rushed a school of mullet. The place and the time and the
action and flash of life united to give this morning's adventure an all-satisfying fascination.

"Lots of fish, an' some busters," remarked Thad. "But
we're late. They won't hang here long."

"We'll hook one in five minutes," said King.

These matured men, fishermen all their lives, were eager
and keen to see the sport begin. I had hardly settled back
in my chair, to compose myself and really take time to
sense things, when a fish took my line out steadily and
evenly. When the slack was about gone I stood up, while
R. C. hurriedly reeled in his bait. Suddenly my fish rushed.
I put on the drag and struck. The hook caught and the
line tightened. My rod was jerked down. My reel
whizzed. Then the water cracked and up shot a beautiful
tarpon, high into the air, turning clear over, and plunging
back. He came out again, and then a third time, which
leap was so spectacular as to elicit yells from all of us.

Then he plugged under the surface, giving me some
trouble to keep him from getting too much line. By dint
of hard pumping and winding I led him back near the
boat. Soon he took another run, swifter and longer than

CURLEW AS THICK AS BEES

NOTE THE BLACK-TIPPED WINGS

the first, at the end of which he leaped and threshed and plunged, tumbled out and back. I took advantage of this effort he had made, and while he was tired from his gymnastics I pumped and reeled as hard as the tackle would stand. He contested the matter with me and for a while longer it was give and take. Half a dozen times he plunged partly out, wagging his head, spreading his gills. At last I brought him to the boat, where Thad pronounced him over one hundred pounds.

Soon the rolling and swishing of tarpon began again, though not quite so often. R. C. had the pains of going through bite, run, hooking, and pulling on a fish—only to find it a shark. Presently a tarpon rolled opposite us, some forty feet out. King took R. C.'s rod, reeled in the bait, and cast it precisely in the spot where the foam bubbles marked the rise of the tarpon.

"Like as not he'll take that," said King.

And sure enough, in a moment I was amazed and excited to see a swirl on the water, and then the shiny, transparent lobe of a tarpon tail rise into the air.

"He's got the bait!" called Thad.

"Just like a bonefish," ejaculated R. C. "What do you know about that?"

I did not feel sure the tarpon had R. C.'s mullet until the line began to run out. My brother struck him just as I dove for the big camera. This tarpon leaped before he ran. He shot up clean, nimble, curved as a bow, silvery bright, dripping diamonds and pearls. Crash! He went down, only to rush to the surface, beating and churning it into foam; and then running far, he burst out again, flashing in the sunlight. Far from us he gave a fine exhibition of leaping, dancing, tumbling. When that was over he went under and fought hard, making it necessary for us to follow him in the boat, while R. C. worked strenuously. This tarpon showed something of the gameness and endurance that have made the Silver King famous. He led us all over our fishing ground, routed out the other tarpon, and gave up only after a half hour's resistance. The boys pronounced him about one hundred and twenty-five pounds in weight. He was hooked on the outside of the mouth, which fact prompted us to release him. He swam off with alacrity, considering all he had endured.

We returned to the favored spot and cast out more baits. But the tarpon had gone on the rising tide. The bar upon which we had beached our boats was thickly encrusted with oysters, growing in clusters. King collected some for us, breaking what he called fat ones from the lean; and he opened several to show us what fine, wholesome oysters they were. Heretofore the only attention we had paid to these oyster beds was a fear that we might cut our lines on the sharp shells. The incident was an illustration of how easily facts of interest and benefit can be missed.

V

A HOUSEBOAT passed near where we rode at anchor, some time late in the morning, and entered the main channel of Broad River.

We remembered this incident in the afternoon, when the strong breeze bore down on us the pungent odor of burning brush and a pall of blue smoke. Captain Thad informed us that hunters from the houseboat had set fire to the saw-grass and hammocks of the Everglades, for the purpose of driving out deer and other game to shoot. He said it was a rather common practice. And I replied that I considered it a cruel and unsportsmanlike way to hunt. Again I had forced upon me the appalling crudeness of the majority of men who seek diversion in remote and wild places.

We fished from four o'clock until sunset, all of which time was unpleasant, owing to the smoke that rolled down out of the Everglades. It made my eyes smart. It made impossible the taking of pictures. The dull red sun set through a purple veil.

Captain Thad rowed me back to the launch, and then returned across the narrow bay to the shoals where King was casting his net for mullet. The short twilight failed and dusk stole down over the islands and the waterways between. Near where the launch was anchored narrow oyster beds stood out above low tide and connected with a line of islands that reached in to the main forest. A great flock of pelicans came flying out of the gloom to alight on the bare oyster beds. From there they flew in continuous stream to the mangrove island near me. A huge round clump of mangroves appeared to be their objective, above which they sailed round and round. I grasped the fact then, that this island was a pelican rookery. The whole flock settled down on the branches, then suddenly took wing again, to fly and sail around and repeat their first performance. They did the same thing again. It seemed to me they were afraid of something. It hardly could have been my nearness, as apparently they took no notice of me or the launch. Despite their undoubted excitement, they were noiseless. Indeed, they seemed ghosts of weird birds in the semidarkness. I felt inclined to believe there was an enemy hidden in the mangroves of the rookery. Captain Thad had told me that there were both wildcats and panthers in the glades. They certainly had to be good swimmers.

We planned to fish the same place next morning and take advantage of the later tide. Naturally we indulged in keen anticipations. But, alas, for the hopes of fishermen! I was up before six to find the wind blowing cold and hard. Nevertheless, we went, and sat for hours in the raw breeze. A few tarpon rolled just before the last of the ebb. On the rising tide, which should have been the best time, we did not see a fish. Whereupon we returned to the house-boat with the idea in mind of going up Broad River for a day or two.

From the deck of the *Ladyfish* the scenery at the entrance of this archipelago was remarkably beautiful. Islands and channels resembled a checkerboard with all the spaces rounded irregularly. Soon we left the grim, impenetrable, iron wall of mangroves for a gradually softening and diminishing forest cover. The main channel was swift and tortuous, and that, with the strong wind from the north, gave Captain Thad all he wanted at the wheel. It was not long, however, before we entered Broad River proper, and it appeared to be felicitously named. I spent the time sitting out on the bow, interested in the gradual change of foliage. Mangroves were still much in evidence, but vastly less, and their omnipresence was diminished by palmettoes and buttonwoods and live-oaks and other trees I could not name. The ground upon which this jungle grew appeared to have become stable, no longer mud full of crab holes. It not only supported the thick forest, but also a wonderful growth of ferns, vines, and grass. Some of the ferns were as high as a tall man; the vines wound

CURLEW RELUCTANT TO LEAVE THEIR ROOST

SPLITTING THE WATER WHITE

around trees. Orchids and other parasitical growths lent color and strangeness to this jungle.

At intervals we passed breaks in this forest land through which we could see out into the Everglades. Level prairie land of brown sedge, somehow compelling, stretched far as eye could see. Lonely palmettoes dotted the expanse, and here and there a dark-green patch of trees—a hammock.

About ten miles up Broad River we entered a large fair bay bordered by low green forest. This point was as far as the houseboat could go. We anchored there and took to the small boats, in which we penetrated miles beyond the open bay, into winding creeks.

I was struck by the absence of birds and wild fowl. Perhaps this fact was owing to the prairie fire started by the hunters on the other houseboat, that had penetrated this region the day before. Huge columns of purple smoke were still rising in one quarter. We saw a few scattered tarpon roll.

Toward the narrowing end of a crooked waterway we came upon a canoe—a dugout, hollowed from a tree— moored at a dark portal into the green depths of forest, and as we turned shoreward in our curiosity an Indian appeared. It was highly interesting to meet a Seminole in his native haunts, and we ran in to shore and engaged him in conversation.

He was not a young Indian by any means, or striking in any way. He wore an old auto cap and blue jeans. He was barefooted. How unromantic a contrast he presented to the vivid, colorful figure I had in mind! Seminoles are noted for their brilliant garb.

He had rather a pleasant face, somewhat of a cast

similar to a Japanese. Nothing of the dark, somber features of a Navajo or Apache. He spoke some English fairly well.

In a little clearing some rods back in the jungle I espied blue smoke of a camp fire, and several dead alligators lying on the ground. He said he had killed eleven the night before.

Captain Thad had hunted alligators as a boy and had made a business of it when a man, and he said the Seminole hunted at night, using a torch. He was thus enabled to see the eyes of the alligator shine like balls of green fire. Then he would shoot it with a rifle and seize it before it sank.

Indians have always been of absorbing interest to me, and as we went on our way I looked back to see this Seminole standing in his canoe, watching us. Somehow he seemed a sad figure—a part of the strange race that was perishing. A vanishing American in the Everglades! It seemed so absurd and sentimental for me to pity him. He was content and self-sufficient. Nature saw to his needs. Altogether sight of the Seminole roused in me a desire to know more about him and his kind, and the mysterious home they found in the Glades.

VI

MANY treacherous oyster reefs bar the entrance to Lost-man's River. At low tide they stand out in narrow, black, ugly lines in close formation; and at high tide they are hidden—danger shoals known only to those familiar with the coast. They were like iron-toothed fences.

The main channel of the river ran out between

picturesque capes, remarkable for a bit of open grassy land, and a winding strip of white beach so attractive to the eye otherwise repelled by scarred straight walls of mangroves. Shacks on both of these points attested to the fact that fishermen were of heroic mold and could live anywhere. One of these dwellings was made of thatched palm leaves, and, set back a little way from the beach, it had a primitive, almost a savage appearance.

We passed this habitation on our way to another mouth of Lostman's River, farther to the west. It was a series of rough little channels between scrubby mangrove islands; and the tide was so low we had to anchor the launch and take to the skiffs. Then it was a matter of hard rowing.

At length we entered a good-sized creek and came to a large pool where Captain Thad and King expected to find tarpon. But there were none. More and more our tarpon fishing had begun to resemble a stalk, like in hunting big game. We had to find the fish.

We rowed up this creek between spreading mangrove foliage that leaned out farther over us as we advanced. The muddy green water changed to brown and grew clearer. It was the prettiest creek we had entered, though apparently devoid of birds or fish. And it grew shallow, and so narrow that the long leaning branches nearly met. Through this lane we rowed and poled, proceeding more out of stubborn determination to find tarpon than from any hope to fish in such a creek.

When we came to a point where the creek split round an island R. C. and King took the right fork, while Captain Thad and I continued on the left, and we were presently delighted to glide out into a sunny open stretch of amber creek, shaded along the banks by drooping foliage.

Thad saw the fin of a tarpon, and I discerned the well-known circling ripple of another. Next we ran right alongside a sleeping tarpon, just under the surface. He looked green and gold. Thad splashed at him with an oar. What a surge and roar he made! Then we saw the break of one close ahead and the wave of another farther on.

We heard R. C. and King before we could see where their creek joined ours. They were splashing at a great rate. Presently they appeared round a green corner, both standing up, poling with oars.

"Hey! there's tarpon here!" called King. "We'll chase them down to the pool."

The water was growing shallow. It had the color of clear hemlock water of the mountains of Pennsylvania or New York. Our companions turned in ahead of us and at once began to point our tarpon and to splash at one here and there. These fish passed us, swift pale gleams.

"Hear them?" shouted Thad. "Listen. Sounds like a gun-shot far off."

Just before that I had heard what certainly seemed like the report of a gun. But it was a noise made by a tarpon under the water. I listened with keener ears.

"There's some more!" yelled King.

"One's a whale!" yelled R. C.

I saw waves in the water ahead, and then arrowy gleams that sped by. Thrumm! Thrumm! The sound was distinct and heavy, absolutely new to me and very thrilling.

"There's a bunch comin'," called Thad.

By peering intently down I espied one big tarpon making the swift tail movement that produced the deep, hollow sound. No wonder! It had great power, and was indeed a singular flip of a fish tail. Both Captain Thad and King averred that the tarpon was the only fish which could make it. I believed, however, if other large, swift fish could be met in such shallow water, they might make this thrumming sound. It would be even more interesting, to be sure, if the tarpon alone was able to do it.

The water shoaled until it was scarcely three feet deep, and the fish our comrades frightened shot by us in plain sight. Many thirty, forty, fifty-pound tarpon, and some big ones, made furrows in the water as they passed. They were as quick as minnows. I had not known before this what a shy fish the tarpon was.

We went as far up the creek as we could force our way under the mangrove branches, and we routed out tarpon by the score. Then we turned back, and proceeded to splash and pound on the boat.

In due time we arrived at the turn of the creek where it widened into the large pool. Here, to our great satisfaction, tarpon were rolling and breaking in numbers to excite us with extravagant hopes. Taking up stations opposite each other we began to fish, assuredly with the strange fallacy that possessed fishermen.

The tarpon rolled and broke and puffed, then settled down for a while, and again rose to the surface. All around the pool and in the middle they surfaced, lazily and sluggishly. But never one of them bit! This waiting game, from being thrilling, became tantalizing, and finally unendurable. Four hours we waited! The tide flooded and began to ebb. The tarpon, as if to bewilder us further, stayed in the pool, contrary to their usual obedience to the tides. They were punishing us for routing them out of the clear, sun-flecked, quiet creek above. At last I gave up, more convinced than ever before that tarpon were shy, sensitive, capricious fish.

Next morning we entered the main channel of Lostman's River, and wound a zigzag course to get by the bars and the capes into the great bay that opened beyond.

I was to learn that Lostman's River did not really begin until we had traversed the chain of bays. The first of these was three miles long, almost as wide, and bordered by irregular shore lines of bright green. Channels and bays followed, one after another, for half a dozen miles. The water began to take on the brownish cast peculiar to the Everglades. I saw no ducks or fish or birds. We came at length into a region of islands of every size and shape. And after a run of two hours we reached the last bay, a large, beautiful sheet of brown water with low shores of green. The surface was smooth and shining, scarcely rippled by the gentle breeze. Tarpon were rolling all about, some of which appeared the largest we had seen. As we were on the way to find a big rookery, we did not tarry to try conclusions with the tarpon, feeling that, as we had discovered them we could come back.

At the upper end of this long bay we entered what Captain Thad called old Lostman's River; and for two hours more we did little else than turn bends in a bewilderingly crooked and narrowing stream. The rookery we sought no longer existed and, much disappointed, we kept on and on, beyond the last patches of mangroves bordering the creek out into the real Everglades.

I found this a recompense for the much longed-for sight of another rookery of birds. We kept on until the boats stuck in the mud in a creek scarcely fifty feet wide, bordering the creek, running out into the Everglades.

For the first time I was powerfully impressed by this strange region. The vast prairie lands and deserts of the West I knew well. This was the Everglades. I could not see the felicitousness of its name, but acknowledged something of charm. Evergrass would have been truer. Far from the low margin of the creek, far as my gaze could grasp, stretched a level plain of saw grass, a sedge resembling cat-tails, greenish brown in hue. Here and there a lonely palmetto dotted the landscape, and far on, in the dim haze, showed patches of trees, or a group of palmettoes. Wild fowl winged wavering flight over that wasteland.

It was summer. Heat veils rose from the prairie. A soft breeze blew hot in my face, bringing the scent of dry grass and distant swamp and far-off fragrance of flowers. No lonely solitude of desert ever equaled that wilderness! Low, level, monotonous, it spread away endlessly to north and east, for what I knew to be far over a hundred miles. It was the home of wild fowl and beast and alligator, and the elusive Seminole. Gazing across this waving sea of grass, I had a conception of the Seminole's hatred of all that pertained to the white man. The Everglade Indian must love this inaccessible, inhospitable wilderness that was neither wholly land nor water. He was alone there. No white man could follow him. The last three hundred of his race would die there, and perish from the earth.

Wild places had always haunted me. Yet I had not anticipated any lure of the Everglades. But something seized me—the old passion to wander, to travel on foot, to seek, to find, to fight obstacles. And the insurmountable obstacle of the Everglades laid its strange hold on my imagination.   No white man had ever mastered this wild country.

Yet, strong as my feeling was, I would not have wanted to roam long over the Everglades. I wanted to penetrate a few miles, by my own exertions, and satisfy a strong curiosity. Here I felt no longing for the unattainable.

A great snowy crane—the egret—winged lumbering flight across my vision, and I followed him until he was lost to view low down in the west.   Of all wild birds the egret had been most hunted by men.   Hunted for the exquisite white plumes that decorated the female at the nesting! I certainly did not mark the flight of this wild fowl to do it harm.   Rather with wonder at its beauty and sadness for its unhappy fate.   Beauty is an unending joy, yet in many ways it pays a terrible price.

This border of Everglades was about twenty miles, as a crow flies, from the coast.   Yet it might as well have been a thousand.   Here was the sedgy portal of the unknown.   I had come to the Ten Thousand Islands and the Everglades to fish and to photograph.   And I was finding myself slowly awakening to a profound realization of the tremendousness of this last and wildest region of America.

All during the long ride down through lakes and lanes I felt the oppression of the truth.   The Everglade region was great through its aloofness.   It could not be possessed. It would continue to provide terrible sanctuary to the fugitive from justice, the outlaw, the egret hunter.   Assuredly the Seminole had been absorbed by it, as proven by his lonely, secretive, self-sufficient existence.

All the way down the hot breeze blew on my face, with its tidings of inscrutable things.   And as I pondered I

TARPON IN TENTH JUMP

TARPON CAUGHT ON LIGHT TACKLE MAKE GREAT COMMOTION WHEN LED
TO THE BOAT

TARPON HEADING UP CREEK

watched the huge horseflies that swarmed like bumblebees round our speeding boat. They flew like a humming-bird. They had the speed of a bullet, the irregular flight of a bat. They were of many sizes and colors, and some were truly wonderful. I saw one fully two inches long. It alighted on my knee. It had a purple head, amber wings, and a body that beggared description. It was veritably the king of all flies, beautiful, yet somehow hideous. I shuddered as I saw it feeling for a place to bite through my clothes. Finally I hit it with my hat—knocked it down hard in the boat; yet it buzzed up and streaked away, high in the air. The everglades bred that fly; and there seemed something significant in the fact.

Upon our return to the big bay we found that a brisk breeze had ruffled the water, putting an end to the rolling of tarpon. Therefore we continued on down the channels, back to the houseboat. Along the coast the wind was blowing hard. During the night it increased, and morning disclosed muddy water. As we could not fish, we rested and wrote notes and worked over tackle.

As the wind was northwest, we were rather fearful of more bad weather, and as we had experienced almost noth-ing but bad weather (from the standpoint of Californians) for more than two months, we were inclined to be peevish. But toward sunset the wind died away.

The sun went down in a golden red-tinged glory, with the clouds on fire and the sea shimmering like an opal. During the night the air grew warmer. I awakened several times, to become aware of the oppressive silence and the heavy atmosphere. Long before sunrise I was up, patrolling the deck. A silvery mist, almost as thick as fog, obscured water and shore line. By and by I caught a glimpse of the dim, shadowy mangroves. Then through the opaque gloom the sun appeared, pale and spectral. It was a sunrise such as I remembered seeing so often in the tropics. This one, however, lacked the accompaniment of the music of wild fowl and parrots and song birds. There was not a sound, except the very faint lap of water against the boat. I was curious to hear what bird would first give evidence of having awakened, and to that end I lent my ears. Gradually the sun brightened to silver, and the mist began to dissolve, and a cool, dewy, balmy spring morning was at hand.

Half an hour later the sun shone hot and a cloudless blue sky beamed down upon us, as with launch and string of skiffs we skimmed away for the day's fishing. It turned out to be an ideal day, like summer, and not wanting in fishing thrills. I caught one tarpon of about seventy-five pounds. When hooked he made three leaps right at the boat, clean, sharp, straight jumps like those of a Marlin, and the last one just missed the skiff. He splashed water all over us and thumped the keel as he shot under. I was reminded again that tarpon have more than once leaped into boats, to the peril of boatman and angler. I had my action planned in case one came aboard, and it was to go the tarpon one better on a leap. At Tampico I saw a huge tarpon sail up into the air and turn over to come down in a head dive, right into the skiff. He knocked the bottom out and went almost through. I was not likely to forget his tremendous flounderings until he freed himself, or the frantic actions of the three men in that boat.

R. C. was out of luck, as the boatmen said. It appeared he had not had a strike for a long time; and from his dejected attitude I gathered that he felt he never would get one.

We made a rather long run to a place called Thickahatchie Bay. The only difference between this bay and a hundred others all around it was that it was larger. My impressions of endless bays and winding channels surrounding innumerable islands were growing weak from overwork. It seemed I had seen all the Ten Thousand Islands of this region. The error was not in the number I had seen, but in the name. It should have been designated by a hundred thousand instead of ten.

In some of the coves of bays adjacent to Thickahatchie Bay we found tarpon rolling, and leaving the launches we poled around in skiffs, hunting for favorable grounds. As in bonefishing, the fact of having located tarpon did not mean we would find a good place to fish for them. There must not be any current, or a rocky or grassy bottom. Usually it took time to discover this; and in fact before we had satisfactorily located ourselves the day was done. We had, however, found an ideal string of coves, in some of which were large tarpon. I had one strike this day, and the fish came up with a heavy crash, showing half his broad body. Before I could wind in the slack, and jerk, the tarpon had thrown the hook. As good luck would have it, however, R. C. had used his camera to advantage.

"I sure snapped that bird," he called to me. "Some fish! Too bad you didn't hang him."

Captain Thad decided this fish would weigh around one hundred and eighty; and he also said that there were bigger fish than that in these coves.

Then, in sun and wind, we had the long run back to the houseboat, turning so many green coves and crossing so many bays that I was hopelessly lost. The islands were covered with a low, brushy mangrove, very bright and symmetrical, and did not have any resemblance to the great grim forest wall down the coast. These islands were some miles in from the coast. But as a matter of fact the coast up this way was all islands.

The following morning we went back to our promising coves. Taking to the skiffs, we paddled along, looking for fins or breaks on the surface. We were not long in finding them and they showed at the mouth of the first cove.

Soon we were anchored at the most favorable points, for the time being—R. C. at the corner of an island and I out some few hundred feet. The day was perfect, warm, still, bright, like summer. A few scattered tarpon were rolling now and then, waiting for a change of tide to work back into the coves. There was something most satisfying in the time and the place. It would have been impossible for me not to be excited and thrilled in such an environment, with big silver tarpon rolling out so close I could pitch a bait upon their backs.

"There's one made a swirl over the bait on your little rod," said Thad. "I reckon he'll do business. You'll sure have a job with that mosquito tackle."

One of my light tackles was really too light, but as we needed several rods to each skiff I was risking this five-and-a-half-ounce tip. The reel was a 3-0—full of No. 9 line. And when I saw this line start to move slowly away from the boat I had quite a second of panic.

"He's got it," said Thad.

TARPON TRYING TO HANG HIMSELF ON MANGROVES

MAKING FOR THE OUTLET TO THE SEA

GULLS ON THE WING

PELICAN ROOST

I whistled our signal to R. C. and took up the rod and rose to my feet. Then the line stopped. I waited. Nothing happened for what seemed ages. Suddenly a silver blaze flashed in the water not ten feet from the boat; then followed a boiling swirl and bulge.

"He's picked up your bait and comes right at us," said Thad. "He saw the boat. Look out!"

I was tinglingly aware that the tarpon had swirled right under our noses, but I had no hope that he still held the bait. All in an instant my line hissed away through the water. Swiftly as I could throw on the drag, I still was not quick enough to jerk before he leaped. He went ten feet into the air, a deformed, convulsive fish shape, all silver and spray. Then as he crashed back I got the slack line in and hooked him, careful even in my excitement not to break the light rig.

My reel screeched, the line hissed out, the little rod wagged. The tarpon burst out with a crack, and throwing himself high he turned clear over in the air, gills and mouth spread so wide that I saw the sky through them. I heard him shake himself like a huge dog. Then he plunged down. But only to shoot up again, straight, broadside to us, mouth shut—a most beautiful sight. He dropped back with a loud smack, furiously churned the water, and was up again, gleaming in the sun.

"Some jumper, I'll say," shouted Thad. "Reckon we'll have to follow him."

R. C. yelled, as was his wont, every time he snapped a picture. As for me, all I could do was to hold the wagging rod and watch the tarpon leap. He was certainly an active and nimble fish. In the ten seconds or more following, while Thad wound in the other line and pulled up anchor,

the fish leaped sheer and high five more times, with as
many crashing lunges on the surface.

This performance altogether ran off two hundred yards
of my line. If he had not sounded then he would have
hung himself on the mangroves. But he went down, and
while I pumped and reeled as hard as I dared, Captain
Thad backed the skiff on him. I had to look up all the
time at the alarming bend of the little rod, lest I pull a
fraction too hard and break it. The strain on me was as
severe as if I had been pulling on heavy tackle. I worked
so hard that I turned the tarpon away from the dangerous
mangroves, and when he swept out into the mouth of the
bay I was tremendously relieved.

"Looks good to me!" ejaculated Thad. "I was some
worried there—about that mosquito rod. But we've a
chance now. And there's R. C. layin' for him with a
camera. He's due to bust out again."

Not until we reached fairly deep water did my tarpon
enter upon his second series of leaps. I had not expected
much. But he amazed and delighted me. If he had been
tired it must have been from his first leaping, for all the
strain I could put on him had not been felt. He tumbled
in and out of the water like a gigantic silver leap-frog.
Straight at R. C.! This was too good to be true. Yet it
could not be denied. He danced over the frothy water; he
wagged up and plunged down; he made of himself a silver
blur. And with a last effort he smashed out right in
front of R. C. and twisted himself all out of shape—to
souse back with a sullen sound.

"Don't let him get rested now," said Thad.

My task, then, was to fight the tarpon with all I and
the tackle could stand while Thad rowed after him. The

spectacular part of the battle was apparently over.   In all I was forty minutes subduing this tarpon, though the time seemed brief.   My left arm was numb, and my hand so stiff I could hardly shut it.   Also I was out of breath and wet with sweat.   We judged the fish would weigh well over a hundred pounds.

When we were all settled again I was glad to rest, and devoutly hoped R. C. would be the one to get the next bite.   The tarpon, however, had worked away from the immediate vicinity.   Captain Thad was in no more of a hurry to follow them than was I, but R. C. and his boat-men crept along close to the mangroves, crossed a couple of channels, and worked up into a quiet cove, where we could see lazy tails and slow ripples and patches of foam and widening circles.

In the succeeding hour R. C.'s thrilling whistle brought me to my feet, camera in hand, four times.   Sharks!   It was most exasperating; and the language that floated across the quiet space of water was humorous and other-wise.   The last shark was about seven feet long, so big and strong that our comrades had to up anchor and follow him.   This was bad business for our tarpon fishing.   Finally R. C. got back most of his line, and at the risk of his light tackle dragged the shark to the boat.   Ordinarily, in a situa-tion like this, the shark would set up a great splashing and floundering, which would spoil any further tarpon fish-ing there.   It was interesting to see King reach the leader, pull the shark close, and, grasping its tail, lift the beast out of water and cut it off.   King was a mullet fish-erman, used to having his nets fouled by these sharks, and he knew how to serve them.   This one did not make even a little splash.

We moved up into the cove, taking a position across the other skiff. The tarpon fell into one of their inactive spells, showing but seldom.

"Reckon they'll soon begin to move round on the flats," said Thad.

I heard the shrill notes of a fish-hawk and searching round, finally located him some distance out over the bay. He appeared to be larger than an osprey, though the white breast and speckled brown back and wings and the small head made him resemble his wilder and rarer brother. This one was fishing. He flew round in a narrow circle, swooped up a little and stopped, with his wide wings beating the air. His position then was wonderful. His white breast was straight up, instead of level with the water, as might seem a natural position, and his tail pointed down. His head was bent forward and down. Maintaining this fluttering standstill for perhaps ten seconds, he then abandoned it and flew away on another little circle, to repeat the performance.

Suddenly he turned over sidewise and pitched down, with wide wings bowed. He gained momentum as he dove and his wings closed in to his body. Like a white streak he shot down, to hit the water and go out of sight. Reappearing, he flew up, shook himself thoroughly and swooped aloft to begin again the circling over the water. What a persistent, patient, inevitable sort of fisher he was! For him it was a matter of life or death. Nature had equipped him perfectly, yet he had to labor incessantly for his life. If fish had been scarce I imagined he might have worked that way day after day, for days, before he had a meal. But here in this bay fish were abundant. I watched him make ten dives into the water, each of which was fruitless. On the eleventh dive, however, he did not come up so quickly or in the same manner. When he did rise it was plain something dragged at him. He had to make tremendous efforts to lift himself clear of the water. I distinctly heard the beating of his wings. But he managed it; his long legs came out, and in his talons wiggled a large shining mullet, fully three pounds in weight. Almost it was too heavy and too strong for the fish hawk. He sagged under the burden, then gathering more power he flew up, and appeared to be equal to the occasion. My further good fortune consisted in the fact that he flew toward me, and passed me some few hundred feet distant and at rather low height. I could see the mullet quivering. I could see the cruel talons gripping the prey. What a wild eagle-like picture silhouetted against the sky! He flew on out of sight beyond the mangroves, perhaps to a nest of little fish hawks, or surely to a perch in a dead mangrove top, where he would rend and devour this prey. By the sea the fish hawk lived.

"Somethin' doing over there," said Thad, interrupting my contemplations.

R. C.'s whistle followed, and I wheeled in time to see him rise and extend his rod. I saw the line rise out of the water, from a point near the skiff out to a distance of thirty yards. It strung taut. Then R. C. jerked hard. A running wave appeared on the surface of the water. It swelled and burst with a roar. A huge silver head waved up, wreathed in white, with great jaws spread V-shaped. There followed a loud tussling sound. Bait and leader flew high into the air. The tarpon had ejected the hook. With slow surge the huge head sank.

"Awww!" cried R. C. in most poignant distress. "He was a whale. Did you see him? . . . Oh, what a fish!"

He slammed the rod hard down in the skiff and stood a moment staring at the widening circles where the tarpon had disappeared.

"Cheer up, R. C.," I called. "It was hard luck, but you've lost bigger fish than that."

Despite my philosophy, however, the glamour of the wonderful day darkened. It was nothing really to lose a great fish. Yet the old boyish emotions were paramount. Never could it be otherwise. R. C.'s bad luck persisted. Always it had taken courage and intelligence to stand against his monumental misfortunes. He sat or rather drooped a while, and then presently he took up the discarded rod and was soon fishing again.

We remained there, faithful to the chance of a strike, until the tarpon worked slowly out into the bay, rolling less and less, and time came when we no longer saw them. Then we rowed back to the launch and were soon speeding down through the chain of bays. R. C. laughed about the big tarpon, and took the ill luck vastly more tranquilly than I.

Once more I attended to the myriads of wild fowl and the changing of channel, island, and bay. And it chanced that I saw a number of fish-hawks. It really must have been fish-hawk day. Most of them were poising above the water, or flying around, watching for a mullet on the surface. I saw several dive, but at too great a distance for me to mark the result. Presently one appeared flying heavily, carrying a long object in its talons. As it approached I was amazed to see the object was a rather heavy crooked stick of wood. This fish-hawk was build-

ing a nest. Not long after that I espied another standing
on the edge of a huge nest in the top of a high dead
mangrove. As we passed, the bird took notice of us, then
resumed its former actions, which I perceived to be the
tearing of a fish it held in its talons. I strained my eyes
to see if it was feeding young hawks in the nest, but I
could not be certain.

VII

THE endless monotony of this level low country had a
strange irritating effect upon my mind and nerves. I
could not live long in a region where there were no hills.
Often I found myself conscious of a longing to climb one
of the high mangroves. I had acquired a habit, too, of
ascending to the roof deck of the *Ladyfish,* apparently to
walk and feel the breeze. But as a matter of fact it was
to get as high as possible.

Back in the Everglades the ground rose to several feet
above sea-level. It appeared to me that a very high tide
would inundate the whole prairie land. It was marsh land,
a swamp, with deceiving dry grassy plots. Therefore,
when I saw the mounds at Chockoloskee, and along
Thickahatchie Bay, I viewed them with quite extraordinary
wonder and delight. Verily they seemed mountains in the
Everglades. The fishing hamlet of Chockoloskee was
located on an island of oyster shells, in some places having
hills of shells thirty or perhaps forty feet above sea-level.
I looked at these little mountains and climbed them with
an infinite appreciation of their singular meaning. Along
Thickahatchie Bay I examined mounds of shells still higher
than at Chockoloskee. Whence their origin? Immediately

I connected them with the thousands of oyster bars and islands, and the millions of mangrove roots incrusted with oysters. Particularly in the Thickahatchie archipelago did these oysters thrive; and in some localities the size of the oysters was prodigious. I saw oysters nearly a foot long. We gathered bushels of them and I found them most appetizing and wholesome.

The hills of oyster shells had been made by a race whose origin and life remained shrouded in mystery. They were a race of giants. Bones found in these mounds were of enormous size. For instance, a jaw bone fit easily over the jaw of a big man of to-day.

These barbarians, or wild men, whoever they were, lived mostly upon oysters, and these shell mounds were their graves and their monuments. How strange! It was one thing to read of prehistoric people leaving monuments in Africa, or Terra del Fuego or Arizona, or in the Everglades, and a vastly different thing to see these monuments. I picked up whole shells that had once been held in the great paw of a primitive giant. Still these people must have been comparatively recent. They left nothing but shells and bones, bits of earthen vessels, flints and fireplaces; and in one place a piece of a fishing net made from hair, which fell to dust when exposed to the air.

The Seminole Indians have claimed their forefathers killed this race of giant oyster-fishers. "Big men—no fight!" the Seminoles said. That added to the mystery.

To me the Seminoles themselves presented as much of a mystery, and greatly more of interest, than the primitive race they claimed to have exterminated. I have lived in the wonderful forest land of the Apaches, and know their relation to the stately pines and spruces; I have had opportunity to study the Moki Indians and their pueblos on the high mesas and escarpments of the Painted Desert; and for years I have traveled among the Navajos in Arizona and Utah. Those Indians, particularly the Navajos have had absorbing interest for me. And therefore I have learned something of the subtlety and complexity of the Indian nature. Enough to form a conception of the wonder and mystery of their lives.

No Indians, however, have stirred my imagination as have these Seminoles.

My first sight of more than one of this tribe came unexpectedly as we rounded an island in the bay of Lostman's River, to meet a Seminole family in one of the native canoes or dugouts. It had been made by hollowing out a log and was graceful in design. A trim triangular sail bellied smoothly in the breeze. The man of this family stood up in the stern with a long paddle in his hands. He was young and striking in appearance. At a little distance his colored garb somewhat resembled that of a Scottish Highlander, showing the bare knees. His hair was black as the wing of a raven and his face clear bronze. Two children, boy and girl, sat leaning over the gunwale, staring at us. They were extremely handsome children and certainly disposed to be curious and friendly. Both wore their hair bobbed, probably without knowledge of the prevailing mode among young white people. Their garments had the hues of the rainbow. In front of them sat the mother, gorgeously arrayed. I had one glimpse of a comely dark face before it was averted. We greeted them, to have the greeting returned. I watched the picturesque canoe until it disappeared up one of the channels leading into the mysterious and trackless region they called home.

At the town of Everglades I saw several more Seminoles, three of whom I had opportunity to study closely. The two young men wore the rough garb of the whites, but the young woman was clad in Seminole regalia. She was aware of the curiosity she had aroused and her attitude seemed that of a dignified princess in the presence of inferiors. Indeed, what struck me most forcibly was her proud bearing. She had a rather long oval face, dark, serene, sad, with unfathomable eyes. Her black hair was worn in a bang level with her eyebrows. She was bare-footed, which fact was obvious only when she walked, sweeping along the full loose skirt. Her costume was really the last style one would imagine worn by Indians in a swampy country. It appeared to be made of some print goods, having gaudy stripes of different colors running horizontally. She wore a collar of beads that came up high under her ears and sloped to her shoulders. From the bib of this neckpiece, front and back, silver ornaments hung. As I gazed at her in a sort of fascination I wondered what the desert Indians would think of these dwellers in the Everglades.

The young men impressed me even more favorably. They were lithe, sinewy of build, clean-cut and sharp of feature, in whose fine dark faces there was no trace of the somber look I had grown used to associating with Indians. They had the same proud, aloof bearing characteristic of their woman companion. Altogether my personal impressions of these Seminoles were memorable.

The early Spanish explorers and pioneers found the

Florida Indians to be a noble and intelligent people. During the Spanish occupation these Indian tribes were conquered by a hardier race from the north. This race became known as the Seminoles and thereafter dominated Florida until the war with the whites. The Seminoles living in the remote Everglades to-day are the descendants of the band of Indians that escaped after the close of the war in 1837.

Once the Seminoles were a large and powerful tribe, living in upper Florida and penetrating the wilds of the swamps at the southern end of the peninsula only on their hunting expeditions. Some historical writers claim that the Seminoles hid and succored negro slaves who had escaped from the plantations, without emphasizing the fact that the hunters who were sent by the white planters with bloodhounds to capture the fugitive slaves stole the cattle belonging to the Seminoles and that this led to war. They maintain that in time hybridism resulted from the contact with the negroes. I have heard this assertion of cross-breeding emphatically denied. It may be true and an interesting item of the scientific history of Indians, but it does not greatly impress me. Many of the writers of the present, as well as the government officials of the past, have been cruel toward the Indians. The old story of white aggression to possess valuable lands belonging to the Indians is true in relation to the Seminoles as it ever was in the West.

There was indeed a long and bloody war between the United States government and the Seminole tribe, ending, of course, in victory for the white army, except in case of the few unconquerable Seminoles who preferred to live in the Everglades rather than become captives of the whites and be deported to some arid Western reservation. That pride, that strength of soul, that wild untamableness must have been the spirit which I felt in the Seminoles I encountered.

The descendants of these fierce warriors have dwindled until now there are only a few hundred left, living in small groups of families in palmetto thatched huts. They still live by fishing and hunting. Contact with the whites has been less degenerating than in the case of other Indian tribes. The Seminole braves will imbibe freely of the white man's bottle on occasion, but seldom lose their natural poise and dignity. Some tribal customs are still inviolate. The Indian woman goes off alone into the woods to bear her offspring, and when she returns with her new-born babe she presents it at once for holy offices.

The last of the Seminoles sounds as romantic to me as The Last of the Mohicans. Who shall write the story of the Everglade Indian? It would be the most pathetic and tragic story of all our vanishing native Americans. Who could do justice to the strife and agony of soul, the endurance of this proud wild people? The world moves on, they say—toward progress. But according to the truths of evolution the Seminoles in the eyes of nature are more fit to survive than the white people who have doomed them to the forbidding Everglades. For they are self-sufficient. They can live and endure where the white man would perish. Monstrous injustices are perpetrated in the name of progress. The white race should have been generous to the red, and have absorbed them, instead of robbing them and forcing them to war, to captivity, to exile in waste places.

We traveled miles up one of the winding creeks to the camp of an old Seminole well known to Captain Thad. The place where the shack had stood was deserted, as we perceived from a distance.

The creek forked here, and the smaller branch led back under dense vine-covered mangroves, where the water gleamed dark and still. Silent wild fowl flew at our approach. When we drew close I saw a bare plot of ground, rather like a low mound, surrounded on three sides by the jungle. A leafless gumbo-limbo tree, strange in all that thick foliage, stood like a sentinel at the back of the glade. We ran the launch to the bank and I leaped ashore.

Two bright-colored garments hanging on the tree attracted my attention. They proved to be Seminole gowns of small size, manifestly the discarded apparel of Seminole children. They appeared to be worn out, yet retained something of radiance. I wanted to appropriate one for a souvenir, but in the absence of the owner I refrained.

The place had not been long abandoned, as was evident by the remains of a camp fire. Sticks of dead mangrove had been placed in a circle, like the spokes of a wheel, and had been burned at the hub end. A pile of cane stalks leaned against the tree. Half a dozen flourishing banana plants, fully fifteen feet tall, bordered the back of the glade. A patch of cane, green and fresh, resembling corn, waved in the breeze on the opposite side. And there were some wandering sweet-potato plants among the stalks of cane. I found several sweet potatoes, lying beside the tree, and upon cutting one I saw that it had not yet dried out. It tasted sweet, of a rather wild flavor, not unpleasing and I ate half of it raw. A trail led out behind through the jungle, and I followed it to the mangrove swamp. Faintly through the network of mangroves I descried the open brown waste of the Everglades. Manifestly the jungle confined itself to the creek margins.

Despite the swarms of mosquitoes, I sat awhile under the gumbo-limbo tree, and for a dream moment I snatched at the lonely life of the Seminole. He was a man and he could exist there. I gave him my infinite respect. Man after all is the greatest animal. These solitude-loving Indians had a boat, a tent, a gun, garments for their backs and food enough to subsist on, and the utter loneliness of the Everglades. This camp was just on the edge of the glades, eighteen miles from the coast. The Seminole had but to pole his dugout canoe into the dim jungle-covered creek to be lost from all possible contact with the white man. As a comfort and a sustaining power, perhaps a religion, he had Nature. And Nature there was the same as in any other part of the world. Sun and wind, rain and dew, dry and wet, the hot sultriness of summer and the tempering breezes of winter, myriads of wild fowl, and game and fish, the enchanting hammocks of the interior of the glades, the untrodden and unpaddled wilderness—these were his alone in all the might of a beneficence unknown to white men, in a glory of a kinship with the elements, in the life of the savage as it was intended by the Creator. Who shall deny it beauty, strength, peace, and a happiness not possible in the marts of the world?

VIII

On the afternoon of April 12th we anchored off the mouth of Chatham Bend River, in the lee of the clam shoals. A brisk south wind was blowing, and as a consequence the air was hot and the humidity heavy. It seemed difficult to breathe and the slightest exertion induced a perspiration. Everything was wet and sticky. All of which was ample reason for disliking a south wind.

Toward sundown the wind dropped and in a few moments there was a dead calm. We felt relieved at once. And as the sun gradually lost its brilliance the air grew cooler. A few tarpon rolled near the boat. The soft splash of others too far away to see floated to us in the stillness.

When the sun descended to the bank of clouds in the west there followed a sudden heightening of color. The center of the cloud bank waved in whorls, as if it had been broken up by wind. Beneath the sun they shone gold and yellow and mauve. But when the sun sank behind them they turned cerise, contrasting vividly with the dark purple belt just above the horizon. When the intense light dulled and darkened there was an effect of sullen, angry fire and storm and thundercloud. Soon the sun slid from behind this broken mass, a ball of magenta. As it dipped back of the purple belt it lost fire and became a vanishing disk of pale rose. Then the last curve of rim went out, like a light in the dark. The day was done.

Some moments later a beautiful effulgence gleamed over the water, a shimmering amber and pink, restless, quivering. It was a reflection of the afterglow of sunset on the fleecy clouds above.

Before dusk had really shadowed the sea mosquitoes arrived in force from the mangroves. They arrived ten million strong. It was impossible to keep them out of the saloon, and we were soon driven to our staterooms, which, happily, were inviolate. They darkened the outside of the window screens and kept up a loud whine. I rather enjoyed my safety and the angry hum with which they resented it. Ordinarily mosquitoes never interfered with my activity, if they did sometimes hamper my enjoyment. But in the Everglades mosquitoes must be reckoned with. At times they were terrible. On a windless night like this, if a man were caught out unprotected, they would kill him.

Sometime late in the night I awoke. The dead calm still prevailed. But the mosquitoes were gone. I wondered about that. Then I heard owls hooting. We were anchored half a mile off the mangroves, yet one of the owls, at least, sounded as if he were on the upper deck. His call seemed hardly a hoot. It was a woo-woooo! At least five different owls answered him, for I heard separate calls, each of which was less clear, farther away, weirder, and more of a haunting moan. I sat up in my berth and turned my ear to the window and listened for a long time. Seldom had I heard any lonelier sounds than the moping of owls. Canyon owls especially had a haunting note of solitude and melancholy. But these mangrove owls made my blood run cold. My consciousness of the dismal dark abode where they lived was so intense that I could think of them only as harpies of the desolate Everglades.

Morning came, with a warming red sun and a rising wind. We manned the small launch and, dragging our skiffs, we entered the narrow mouth of Chatham Bend River. It did not look at all like any other river we had explored, but I could not tell wherein the difference lay. I was particularly interested in this river because Captain Thad had told me about the notorious outlaw and gunman who had lived on it. The Everglades had harbored many

SNOOK IN NOSE DIVE. NOTE THE BLACK STRIPE ON SIDE

TROLLING AT MOUTH OF BROAD RIVER

HOOKING THE GAME SNOOK

fugitives and many bad men, and it still held its reputation in such regard, but for daring outlawry Watson stood alone.   In all my study of Western frontier life, embracing countless books, and much travel, and contact with all kinds of desperate characters, I never came across a story of a more tragic end than Watson's.   Some day I may write his history.

I was amazed when I saw the place where Watson had lived so many years.   Naturally, having seen a few dilapidated shacks along these mangrove shores, hidden in almost inaccessible nooks, I had expected Watson's to be the same, even wilder, as befitted the man's career.   But his house was a large, pretentious frame structure, painted, with windows screened, standing on a high open point, and backed by a large tract of cultivated land.   It was as lonely, however, as any shack in the Everglades.

Some ten or twelve miles up Chatham Bend River we entered a wide bay full of oyster bars; and here we went aground so often that I feared we would never find deep water again.   But even shallow water in the Glades had an end.   We got through, and eventually, by devious channels, and tunnels under mangroves, and bends that left no doubt as to the felicitousness of part of the name bestowed upon this river, we arrived at the creek Captain King averred would be full of tarpon.   I ventured to inquire when he had last visited this place.

"Reckon it was aboot nine years ago," he said.   "An' it shore was full of tarpon then.   Some regular he-rhinoceros busters, too."

King's creek opened into a little bay, an ideal retreat for the great silver fish, snug and smooth in the lee of mangroves.   Our diligent survey found only one tarpon.   He was big enough to set us keenly to positions, and tackle and bait. While we were getting ready to deprive him of liberty for a while, perhaps his life, he swam to and fro before us, broad tail and long dorsal above water. No sooner had we got our baits out and a quantity of chum, than the big tarpon got busy. He began to pick up the pieces of fish we had so kindly thrown in his way. Every time he stood on his head in the three feet of water his broad forked tail came clear out. Fish fins and fish tails had a compelling power to thrill and excite me. Moreover, our boatmen were expressing most decided ideas as to the inevitable fact that he was already our tarpon. R. C., himself seldom extravagant, began to calculate the leaps and wanted to bet he would snap so many pictures.

"Shore, he's walkin' to his funeral right now," said King.

"Look at the way he's pickin' that chum," said Thad. "He might just as well swim over here an' give up."

"Hurry and hand him a bait," shouted R. C., impatiently.

Somehow, despite the sanguine remarks of my comrades, I knew that lone tarpon was as safe as if he had been in Lake Okeechobee. He ate up all the chum, swam around and over my bait, and then went to chasing live mullet. He worked away from our position. Once he broke water, showing himself, and he was big and broad and silvery. My companions were ungracious enough to cast slurs upon this beautiful fish.

We abandoned the bay and creek for others no better, and at length turned downstream with the tide. The wind, the glare, the heat made me drowsy, and I fell half asleep. Suddenly I was roused by a yell in my ear.

"Snook! Snook!" R. C. was waving and pointing, as

well as yelling. I was in time to see a school of large snook
swim away from the boat into deep water. The stream took
a sharp turn round a shady point of mangrove. The
current was swift.

We anchored the skiffs and went to trolling with our
light tackles, using spinners. We had not gone thirty
yards before boils and swirls back of our spinners attested
to the rush of snook. R. C. hooked a big one. He came
out and shook himself free. Then I hooked another. He
made a hard run, under the bank and, fouling on a snag,
got away.

"Good chances to snap pictures," I said to R. C. "You
fish. We'll take turns."

R. C. caught two snook of several pounds each, which
we saved to eat. Next he got a fine jump out of a small
tarpon. The water was clear and not unlike that of a fresh-
water stream. In fact, the fishing seemed exactly like that
on an inland river where muskalonge and pike abounded.
A snook resembles a muskalonge in appearance, strike, and
fight. We worked up along the bank, keeping close to the
overshadowing brush and roots and leaves. R. C. had a
strike for every ten feet of the way. Some of the snook
missed the hook; others hit it and threw it; finally a heavy
fellow with a mighty swirl fastened himself tight. He
began to jump, and here was where I took advantage of
opportunity.

R. C.'s tackle was too light for a snook of this size, and
he could not hold or lead him. But luck favored us in this
instance. The snook missed snags, and when he jumped
to hang himself over brush the dead branches obligingly
gave way. This fish took line, making rushes, sulked in
holes, plugged to hang the line on something, and particu-

larly fougl   ı the surface in leaps and long tussling skitter-
ing breaks. He had to be handled with skill and extreme
delicacy, for the mouth of a snook tears easily. In all he
gave an exhibition that thoroughly earned our admiration,
and when R. C. had finally subdued him—and I had photographed him—a pale-gold, gleaming, black-lined fish of
twelve pounds—we returned him unhurt to the water.

That was the beginning of a most extraordinary lot of
fun. We took turns with my rod, after R. C. had broken
his. Certain places along the creek we named appropriately.
The best was Snook Corner. We never failed to hook one
here, and if he freed himself, which two out of three fish
accomplished, there was always another ready to rush the
spinner.

Together we hooked innumerable of these game fish,
some too heavy to hold; and we caught twenty, the largest
of which ranged from eight to twelve pounds. We used
up four rolls of film. And when we were thoroughly tired
out, after three strenuous hours, we quit fishing and went
on our way.

"That was great!" exclaimed R. C.

It did not seem an exaggeration. To fish in a beautiful
place, to see the quarry rush and strike and leap, to outwit
him by skill and strength, to return him unhurt to the water,
sure that there were no sharks to take advantage of his ex-
haustion, and particularly to have the strikes come thick
and fast and heavy—that was indeed all satisfying to my
brother, and no doubt even more to me.

On our return we passed a small mangrove island and
were attracted by sight of a huge nest of eagle or osprey,
black and ragged, in the top of a tree. When we ap-

A FORTY-POUND SNOOK LEAPING TO FREEDOM

THIRTEENTH LEAP OF TWELVE-POUND SNOOK

SNOOK SNAGGING LINE ON MANGROVES

proached, a large fish-hawk left the nest and soared aloft, uttering piercing cries. We soon saw two young hawks, so nearly full fledged that I expected them to fly. But they did not, even when we went close, even when I climbed an adjoining mangrove to obtain a better picture of nest and birds. At last I was inspired to climb to the very top of the tree, so that I stood beside the nest, within reach of the fish-hawks. I was more frightened than they, for I feared the branch would give way under me or the mother bird would swoop down to scalp me with those sharp talons.

The hawks were young, but of almost full size, with breasts of creamy white, and wings, head, and tail of mottled brown. They faced me with what I took for curiosity more than fear. They certainly did not betray any instinct to fly, though they backed to the edge of the nest. What sleek, sharp small heads, eagle-shaped! The eyes were black and orange, the orange being the iris; and the light in them was piercingly wild and beautiful. Wild nature! I did not see hate of man or fear of death in these eyes, as I have seen in older birds of prey. Cautiously I laid a hand on the nearer one, which act excited the bird, though not alarmingly; and then I backed down the tree and returned to the boat. As we left I heard the plaintive cries of the young ones and the piercing reply of the mother. Before we turned a bend she had swooped down to the nest. I wondered what that reunited family would say in fish-hawk language about the intruder.

It occurred to me that I had not failed to take note of the nest. It had been built of dead sticks and was very old, perhaps many years. The under sticks were rotten. The upper were hard wood, indicating that every year a new layer of sticks had been added. The top was almost flat and it was quite solid. I saw no fish bones, and gathered from this fact that the parent birds removed these after every meal. There was a good-sized clump of oyster shells in one place, some of the shells being open. Not unlikely, in lieu of fish the parent hawk had fetched a change of diet. But if so how did she open the oysters?

The next day began with a soft, cool east wind, very delightful. But it dropped early. When we pulled anchor and headed down the coast, the morning was hot. We ran about two hours, and threw anchor at the mouth of another river.

Soon we set out up the creeks to locate tarpon, and before we got well into the mangroves found a round pool where a few fins were showing. We thought to tarry a little while to find out if tarpon were abundant or scarce. Captain Thad baited a rod for me, and while the others watched I fished. Inside of five minutes my line was paying out in a steady strong tarpon strike. I yelled for R. C. to get ready with the camera. But I had scarcely uttered the words when the tarpon leaped, close to the boat. I tried to wind and jerk to set the hook. He leaped again, a long, slim graceful fish, perhaps of a hundred pounds. R. C. was fumbling with my camera—he had not left my boat—complaining frantically that something was out of "whack."

Then with a resounding thump the tarpon slid out and up, almost without splashing, and shot prodigiously high, higher than I had ever before seen a tarpon leap, and turning over he came down head first in a beautiful dive, cutting the water like a blade. In that leap he had thrown the hook. His effort had been so magnificent and spectacular that we were all stunned. When we recovered we all exclaimed in unison. R. C. forgot his chagrin over my camera and I regarded the escape of the fish as freedom well earned. We agreed that when at his highest the tarpon was fifteen feet above water.

After that we rowed up a narrow creek until we found more fish. R. C. soon hooked a tarpon that would not jump. Nor did it at first attempt to go down toward the sea. Space between the mangroves was not more than fifty feet. This tarpon ran off up the creek, making a furrow on the smooth surface. Part of the time he swam under the drooping dead mangroves, breaking off pieces and dragging them along with him. "Good night!" yelled R. C. "We can't hold this bird!"

Captain Thad poled our skiff swiftly up to R. C.'s, jumped into it, and left our engineer, Anderson, to row me. I stood up, camera in hand, but it was hard for me to keep from being lurched overboard, owing to Anderson's heroic efforts to keep up with the other skiff. I had no idea whatever that R. C. would save that fish, but I wanted to see what would happen. He was using a light-tackle rod, but fortunately the reel was equipped with a good fifteen-thread line.

We chased that queer tarpon a quarter of a mile, and all the time he kept a hundred yards ahead of R. C. The boatmen made powerful efforts with oars and pole to gain on the fish. But only the shallow water and narrow space stopped the tarpon.

When he made a tremendous surge around to head down the creek he came right at my boat. I shouted for Anderson to row fast, to this side and that. But it seemed we could not get away from R. C.'s line. It was right under us, to one side and then the other. It caught on Anderson's oars, and what kept it from snapping I could not guess. Finally we got out of the road and let R. C.'s boat by. Then we followed.

"He's got most of my line out again!" yelled R. C. "Row and pole, you buckoos! We're going to catch this bird."

The tarpon took us back down the creek, beyond the point where R. C. had hooked him. My boat was a hundred feet and more behind. I missed several smashes the tarpon made on the surface. I hoped he would leap, but he never did.

The boys overtook him in the wildest place along that creek. It was where a branch ran off to the left, and on that side the water shoaled to a mud bar. Beyond this point was a constriction of the creek, full of snags. In fact, all along the banks, except on the shoal, there were ugly snags sticking up.

"Hold him here, R. C.!" I yelled. "Lick him in this wide place or lose him."

There the real struggle ensued. The tarpon swam, rolled, lunged, and plunged to go on, in any direction. He towed the skiff. R. C. bent that little rod, and when he got the double line over the reel he shut down with both thumbs. Sometimes we were within thirty feet of him. And more than once I had to hold my camera high to keep it from being wet by the tarpon splashing.

"Light-tackle fish, huh!" ejaculated R. C. "Not this bird! I tell you he's strong."

"You're working too hard on him," I called, warningly. "Ease up. Play him safe. It's a big fish."

But I did not observe that my brother heeded my advice. I could see that he was fighting mad. The heat was intense, the mosquitoes and sand flies ferocious. R. C.'s head net had caught in a mangrove branch and had been pulled awry. I could not see his face, but I did not need that to tell he was most uncomfortable. His shirt showed wet with sweat. I was saturated myself and literally being devoured by mosquitoes. My sun glasses fogged with the heat and moisture, and I had to remove them. Then the glare hurt my eyes.

After the tarpon thumped far one way, R. C. would succeed in turning him; and they kept repeating this performance. The tarpon would stick up his nose and puff. Then he would roll, showing a broad gleaming side, gold in the amber water. He worked to one shore and went over and under snags. Then he took a notion to plunge under the skiff. R. C. had a bent rod underwater, clear to the reel, for several moments, while the boys turned the boat. Manifestly this trick appealed to the tarpon, for he essayed it again. R. C. quickly thrust the curving rod down into the water and staggered over seats, around Thad, to clear the stern. Next move of the fish was to make a slow, powerful heave for the west bank. He butted into it, for his nose came out covered with mud. Then, in the center of the widest part of the creek he resorted to the lunges and plunges that plainly gave R. C. the utmost trouble. He had to hold the tarpon, yet not break him off. I certainly appreciated R. C.'s job.

Suddenly the fish amazed me. He made a swift short run. The reel screeched. In such short space he could not be stopped or turned. "Say good-by!" called R. C., grimly.

But the tarpon ran up on the mud bar until he was half

out of water. There he began to wallow. Thad called him a porpoise and King called him a pig. He sent sheets of muddy water flying. He churned and threshed until he slid off the mud. But now, after this last expenditure of strength, he appeared to be weakening. R. C. could turn him, hold him, and at last lead him. Soon after that he rolled wearily on his broad side, blazing in the sunlight, and did not right himself. The battle was over. A few minutes later he was roped to the skiff.

R. C.'s rod had a set curve in it, a deep bend that would never come out. And R. C. himself did not look much straighter.

"Queer fight, wasn't it?" I said, as we came alongside. "I never saw you work harder or better. But of course the conditions made this fight. All the same, he was a game fish."

R. C. was panting as he tore off hat, net, gloves, and threw them down. His face was purple in hue and steaming with sweat.

"How—long—was I—on that—bird?" he gasped.

"Nearly an hour," I replied, consulting my watch.

"Gimme the—water jug.

When he had drunk long he drew a deep breath and wiped his face. "Whew!" he exclaimed, finally. "Shades of swordfish! . . . If I'm not—all in—I'll eat your bait."

Captain Thad slaked a thirst second only to R. C.'s. "I'll say it's hot," he said. "No wonder you're all in. I am, too. How about you, Bob?"

"If we hadn't licked him I'd have been dead by now," replied King. "But ketchin' the durned plugger sort of revived me."

This tarpon was short, thick, broad, and heavy, not the leaping kind. We all guessed at his weight. Thad and Bob, as usual, underestimated it. He weighed one hundred and thirty pounds.

IX

AFTER several full days of tarpon fishing and of adventures encountered while trying to photograph alligators, sawfish, and leaping whip rays, we headed north for Cape Romano.

This cape appeared to be a long narrow strip of rock and sand standing far out into the Gulf. The solid ground was indeed balm for my eyes; and the winding white beach, after the leagues and leagues of grim bright mangroves, positively thrilled me. Rivers and tarpon were the objectives on this trip, but I could not pass by the west shore of Cape Romano.

With launch and skiffs we went round to this shore a considerable distance, for the sole purpose of permitting me to indulge in one of my delights, gathering shells along a lonely beach. I was surprised to find it a real ocean shore, chafed by contending tides. The water was deeper than off Cape Sable or Long Key, where I had passed so many contemplative hours. This shore met the full force of the Gulf and extended along the cape in a meandering line—a wide, shell-ridged beach between sea and mangroves.

What a wild, ragged, lonely shore! Again, and in strangely different place, I was wandering beside the sea, listening to its hollow roar, feeling with rapture its loneliness and beauty. How prodigal the sea had been! Lines

and ridges and piles and patches of shells! I could not
walk without crushing myriads of exquisite, delicate little
shells. They seemed as many as the sands. Close to the
water, on the hard strand, I walked far out along the cape,
and then back. It was a far cry from catching crab bait
to gathering sea shells, but both had their joys. Much as
I loved to fish, and find myself the bait therefore, I believed the possession of a billion sea shells was more to
be desired. My companions hove in sight along the beach,
stooping and bending.

I gathered shells for a whole hour, until I was weary
with stooping, and then I sat down among mounds of glit-
tering jewels of pearl and porphyry, of opal and jasper. I
would pick up a handful, only to discard them for lovelier
ones. Shells of many kinds, of infinite beauty, of innumerable shades and sizes. I made a wonderful collection of
the fluted angel's wings, of the stark whorled shark's eyes,
of the tiny golden conches, of clam shells, buff and creamy
white, purple with white spots, lavender and orange bars,
of the Chinese alphabet, and calico shells, and the pearl
oysters.

It seemed a singularly fascinating thing to sit and kneel
among mounds of shells. With one rake of my hand I
could stir a thousand into musical tinkling notes. The sun
glistened on silver gloss, on dead white bone, on enamel
of rose and amethyst, on transparent opaque glass, on
ridged chalk, pure as snow, on bits of marvelous cerise—
all dainty and delicate shells lost among myriads of other
shells.

They had harbored and protected lives of ocean creatures.
The life was gone and only the untenanted house remained,

TROLLING BETWEEN THE ISLANDS

SNOOK LEAPING AFTER THROWING THE HOOK

TOO SWIFT TO PHOTOGRAPH

the dead structure waiting to be beaten into sands of the shore. Beauty that wasted itself in solitude and loneliness! They held the same meaning that nature always taught— life and use and death and decay for the individual—immortality for the species. Dead shells cast up by the sea! That was the fact, but it did not suffice for me. The magnificent prodigality of the sea, the illimitable range of design and texture, the elaborate painting and sculptoring, the harmonious blending of soft and rich and pure, the appalling beauty—these stirred a pang in my breast, a measureless sadness for the mystery of their little lives, the hopelessness of ever knowing the secret of their origin or understanding the reason for their charm.

While we gathered shells thunder rumbled, the sky darkened, the sound of the sea seemed to swell—and the huge mosquitoes and invisible little sand flies redoubled their efforts to devour us alive before the storm broke.

My indifference to the attacks of these pests was wholly feigned. But it caused my brother a good deal of wonder and chagrin, so I persisted with my deceit. Before the rain arrived there came a cool, strong breeze, most comforting, in that it carried away our rapacious blood-suckers.

To the north and west the sky was purple and black and angry rose and flaming gold, with veils of down-dropping rain. Eastward over the Everglades stood up mountains of white cumulus clouds, majestic and beautiful, as still as if fixed and sculptored marble. Such magnificent clouds rise on extremely hot days over desert and wasteland. These over the Everglades resembled the "thunderheads" that rise from the Mojave Desert, high above the Sierra Nevada range, and can be seen from the Pacific.

Cool scattering drops of rain began to patter about us, and I caught some on my upturned face. How sweet and fresh! Our weeks along the rivers of the Everglades had been hot and dry. We embraced the storm; and when the great raindrops began to fall thick and fast they were most welcome. My hat was full of sea shells, but even if it had been available for wear I should have gone bareheaded.

Only the edge of the storm reached us, yet it was heavy enough to wet us pleasantly and to wash the salty tang from the air.

Captain Thad had for days talked of the next spring tide, which was due early on the morning of April 16. According to him our tarpon fishing had been poor. "Neap tides are no good," he said. "The tarpon go up in the bays and creeks, spread all over, and stay there even on the ebb. But the first spring tide will fetch them out to find deep holes."

I was mighty curious about this prediction of his. He had averred the low tides would come on schedule and the tarpon with them. We were up at four o'clock on the morning of the 16th and a little after five, in the dim, moist summer morning, we manned the small boats and were off up the mouth of the river. We did not get far before we saw tarpon surfacing. We halted there to watch and listen. In the grayness we could hear the souse of a breaking tarpon when we could not see him.

"They're here," said Captain Thad, with satisfaction.

By the time we were anchored, with R. C. a couple of hundred feet from my skiff, and had settled down to actual fishing, day had dawned clear and bright with a rosy sun tipping the mangroves. A track of fire glittered on the water, slowly changing from red to gold. Birds began to sing. And all around us, even on the shoal behind where we anchored, tarpon were rolling. Large fish and many of them! They were light green on the back, showing they were fresh run fish, just in from the sea. But slowly, painfully, the dreadful certainty that they would not bite forced itself into my thrilling waiting consciousness. I saw a thousand tarpon roll lazily, and show their silver sides in the sunlight, and flip their tawny tails. It seemed I heard the breaking splash of many more than that. How often I gazed to where R. C. sat quietly in his boat! Time passed, the sun grew hot, the tide began to get near flood, and the tarpon gradually ceased to roll.

"Queer birds—these tarpon!" called R. C., resignedly.

I was inclined to agree with my brother. "Thad," I said, "what do we know about tarpon, anyway?"

"Nothin'," grunted Thad, in disgust.

"They are not going to bite," I added, voicing my fears.

"Not this tide. Maybe next ebb, if they stay here, an' I reckon they won't."

"Biggest tarpon we've seen yet," I went on, poignantly.

"I saw some that would go close to two hundred pounds," replied Thad, forcibly.

"Let's not give up yet," I concluded, trying to be hopeful.

The tarpon, *Tarpon Atlanticus*, is the most popular game fish of the Gulf states. In these waters it attains a length of seven feet and a weight of two hundred pounds, though but few of the large ones have been taken. It belongs to the herring family and is a giant in size, characterized by its wonderful brilliance of silver, its huge scales, its wide forked tail and feathery dorsal fin, its comparatively small head and big staring black eye, its deep-cut mouth, with the under jaw extending beyond the upper.

Like the salmon and the steelhead, the tarpon goes into fresh water rivers to spawn. At least this spawning theory seems to be proven by the presence of small tarpon at the heads of all the Everglade rivers. But my own observation is that these small tarpon do not appear in great numbers, considering the number of adult tarpon. The boatmen of the west coast claim that a few tarpon remain at all seasons in these rivers; that the fish have been caught every month of the year. But whether or not the same fish stay all year in these waters is something not yet ascertained. My own opinion is that they do not. All sea fish travel, and their habit is to come and go. Toward the end of March and in April the great schools of tarpon run in and out of the Gulf Stream, through the channels between the keys, across the fifty miles of shoals to the Everglades rivers. Bahia Honda Channel appears to be the route most used. Tarpon are caught there in May and June. An old fisherman of Key West told me he had seen a school of tarpon so large that it took all day to pass a given point. In forty years of market fishing he had seen this remarkable run of tarpon only once.

Tarpon work into the mouths of the rivers, according to tides. Mullet, crabs, and small fish constitute their main food. They go in with the rising tide, into the myriads of little inlets and nooks among the mangroves. With the ebbing tide they return, to drop into a deep channel or hole, there to wait for rising tide again. When they are congregated in small area in such places, at slack-water ebb, or the early part of the flow, they are most easily caught. But as Captain Williams averred, you can never be sure

what tarpon will do. All fish have queer moods, and the
tarpon, like the bonefish, are exceptionally finicky. One
thing I absolutely ascertained during this shallow water
angling, is that tarpon are a wary and shy fish. Yet
sometimes they seem bold, indifferent. For the most
part, however, the least jar on the boat or sight of boat will
send them plunging away, raising deep furrows in the
water. They play on the surface, they roll, and they lie
motionless asleep. It is when they roll that a distinct sound
of breathing is heard. Often, after they roll and sink,
bubbles rise to the surface for some yards. Sometimes
they do not show at all for a good while. But I am inclined to believe that if tarpon are in a cove or bay or
channel, sooner or later they will be seen by a sharp pair
of eyes.

By comparison with the tarpon fishing in Mexican waters
I am afraid the Florida and Aransas Pass fishing loses a
good deal. I fished several seasons at Tampico before the
oil wells spoiled the Panuco River for angling. The Panuco at and near its mouth was a wide, deep river of clear
green water. Between the stone jetties there was always a
smooth swell rolling in from the sea, and a current, coming in or passing out. I had many a wonderful day trolling
in this fascinating and dangerous place. It was nothing to
hook a tarpon, except that the strike would lift me from my
seat and nearly jerk the rod out of my hands. But to
subdue a big one was worth remembering. In such water
tarpon have a chance to run and leap. I have had one
two hundred yards and more from the boat for a long hour,
and could neither drag him closer nor row any nearer.
Tarpon grow very large in Mexican waters. My largest
was seven feet five inches in length and broad and thick, a

hump-backed fish that would have weighed much over two hundred pounds. The longest I ever saw was seven feet ten inches. They reach even a greater length, but this one was the record for Tampico.

The man who made this remarkable catch was not a fisherman. He was a whisky drummer from Texas, and when he dropped into Tampico he appeared the worse for his own wares. Poindexter, who managed the fishing trade, gave him an old tackle and a *mozo* who had never rowed for a tarpon fisherman. The anglers present that morning laughed at Poindexter's suave assurances to the drunken man.

Three hours later, as I passed the mouth of a lagoon, I espied this inebriated novice hanging on to a huge tarpon that rolled its head and hump out and appeared to be trying to climb the bank. I had my *mozo* row me around for awhile, in a hope that the tarpon would leap. But it did not; and as there seemed no possibility of the boatman and angler ever beating the fish I went on my way, on down toward La Barra.

Two hours later, on my return, I found, to my amaze, that the drummer was still hanging to the tarpon. I rowed close. He was sober now, and surely a dishevelled and sweaty individual. Stripped to his undershirt, bareheaded and red-faced, mad as a hornet at that tarpon, he surely was a spectacle of an angler. The tarpon had been on six hours and was then towing the skiff. I proposed that the drummer take my experienced boatman, while I took his, and see if they could not beach the fish. The exchange of *mozos* was made, and eventually the great tarpon landed. I did not go ashore, but I saw the huge glistening Silver King from a distance—and that sufficed for me.

At the hotel that evening Poindexter raved in mixed Mexican and English, trying to express his grief over such a magnificent tarpon falling to the luck of a novice. Why could not one of his oldest and best patrons have been so favored by angling fortune? Poindexter did all the raving. The rest of us were silent. That tarpon was as long and wide as a door. Such tarpon do not come north; at least not one has been caught.

X

NEXT morning we were up even earlier, and on the fishing ground where we had located the tarpon, just a little after dawn. None of us really expected the tarpon to be there. But they were. We heard them splashing, sousing, and puffing before we could see them in the dim gray light.

Morning came quickly, a soft, sweet, balmy spring morning, with music of awakening birds all around us and the fragrance of blossoming vines or trees somewhere near. The sun heralded his coming by a pink effulgence in the sky, and soon rose red and gold. The water shimmered like a stream of molten jewels; and everywhere we looked its surface was rippled or broken by rolling tarpon.

An early start and a later tide made conditions better for us than they had been the day before. In fact, the tide had just begun to rise. Only one factor remained to make the experience perfect—and that was for the tarpon to bite.

R. C. was located near a small island where the channel appeared to form a deep eddy. Here dozens of tarpon were rolling. And very soon R. C. called out sharp and clear, "Something doing!"

That was a fair promise for the morning's luck. Fishermen never outgrow their superstitions regarding chance.

A moment more and a splendid tarpon cleared the air, so brilliant and beautiful in the early morning sunlight that he seemed to come from some unreal and fairy-like world. When he crashed down, to leap again on a tight line, R. C. let out a cry that meant the tarpon had not thrown the hook. In and out, up and down, this silver fish flashed until at last, halfway across the channel he wagged out and plunged back. I did not see him again for half an hour when he rolled his head out near R. C.'s boat. He was a big fish and required careful handling.

"Well, what you doing over there?" called R. C.

"We constitute your audience," I replied.

R. C. had scarcely settled down to a comfortable seat when he had another strike. I saw it before he whistled. An instant later my line started out slow, strong, steady. As I picked up my rod Captain Thad said: "By gosh! There's a bite on your other rod!"

That seemed a superfluity of good fortune. But presently it did not look so good. The line on my extra rod was crossing the one I held. I felt the contact. My line ceased to pay out—then it whizzed off the reel. There followed a tremendous splash and a huge tarpon leaped so close to us that he made a great black blur against the sky. As he obscured the sun he actually looked black. But I saw the marvelous outline and the incredible action. The tussle he made somewhat resembled the action of a horse shaking off dust which he had gathered rolling. With a loud live crash he disappeared. And my line was limp! I stared at it.

BIG SNOOK AT END OF RUN

LAGOON IN EVERGLADES

THE EVERGLADE PALMETTO AND SAW GRASS

"Just as well that happened. You've still got another bite," said Captain Thad, handing me the other rod.

I had again the same thrill of expectancy, the same tingling, breathless curiosity. When I struck hard and felt the heavy weight, the sudden lunge on the line, I stared as if fascinated at the space of water where the tarpon should show.

"Shark," said Thad. "Too bad! He ran across your other line and made the tarpon throw the hook. He sure made a flop."

Before a sickening disappointment quite seized upon me I heard the unmistakable rapid flopping of a fish half out of the water. I had forgotten R. C. Wheeling, I was just in time to see a tarpon in a beautiful headlong dive. The next leap was a twisting somersault. After that the fish stayed down. I watched R. C. working on him, bending the little rod. The fish was away fully two hundred yards and fighting doggedly.

"Do you fellows ever follow a tarpon?" I called, sarcastically.

"Reckon we'll wait till we hang a buster. This one'll only go aboot hundred forty-five," replied King, cheerily.

I was certainly delighted to see my brother so fortunately engaged and so blithe about it, but I did not think any too favorably of his risking so much on the light tackle.

"Say, R. C.," I yelled, finally, "if you'd fall overboard what do you suppose you would come up with?"

"Cheer up. You'll catch one some day, maybe," he replied. "Watch me pull this bird's head off."

He did not quite literally succeed in accomplishing his boast, but he managed to whip that tarpon and pull him in, without moving the boat.

Contrary to what we naturally expected, the tarpon continued to roll and sport on the surface.

"You can never tell," said Thad. "Look how they acted yesterday morning. We'll ketch another one, sure, before they work off on the flats."

"That lucky red-head may, but I've a feeling of disaster," I replied.

In truth, I was two persons, a composite of a watcher by the sea, reveling in the glancing, mysterious water as every instant it gleamed here or there with a bar of silver, and an angler glad to be alive, grateful to be there, happy at my brother's good luck, and very peevishly anathematizing my own miserable fortune.

"Hey! Come over here and take my rod," R. C. called, gayly.

I turned to see him standing in the skiff, bending forward, rod extended, in that familiar and thrilling pose I had seen him assume thousands of times since boyhood.

"What for?" I yelled, as if I did not know.

"I just got a bite . . . Watch me hand it to this one!"

I did watch him then, and every instant for a while. I saw him hook and begin to play a still larger tarpon. It made seven leaps clear of the surface, and then, after surging this way and that, turned toward our boat. I got ready with the camera. I was facing the sun, and that was bad for picture-taking. The tarpon appeared so active that I was certain he would leap again.

"Get ready to beat it away from there," called King, warningly.

Captain Thad wound in our lines, and was hauling on the anchor when the tarpon broke close to us. It was like the explosion of a shell. Then he slapped his gills in loud cracks. And that same shuddering, convulsive shaking noise filled my ears. I snapped a picture with the camera focused for one hundred feet when the tarpon had leaped scarce twenty-five feet from us. Swiftly I changed focus. He came out again, farther away, and again I was wrong. The best jump occurred while I was winding a new number into place. I did not see it, but I heard it and the shouts of my comrades. When I faced around the tarpon was down. I saw the line and tried to judge where the fish would again appear. But he fooled me. I figured between fifty and a hundred feet. He split the water close to us again and shot up in a perfect action, a clean-cut leap without wagging, shaking, or cracking his gills. When he went down he was headed for our boat. R. C. was yelling. So was King. Captain Thad shouted warnings—I could not hear what. And I was frantically changing my focus. I just had it done when the tarpon burst out of a caldron of flying white spray, and carrying up a wreath of foam and a rainbow mist, and myriads of diamond drops, he went into the air until his tail was as high as my head. My camera snapped too late.

That appeared to be the end of his aerial performances. But we got out of his way, and standing off at a safe distance we watched R. C. handle him in masterly fashion and at length bring him in. Captain King had to gaff this fish, as manifestly he was too heavy to take care of otherwise. Both he and R. C. disappeared in spray, and most certainly received a good wetting. I could hear King talking to the wrestling tarpon.

"Didn't I tell you we'd ketch you?" he demanded. Captain King was nothing if not a real fisherman.

"Biggest one yet!" called R. C. as he looked over at me, with the light flashing on his face.

That ended our fishing in the channel. The tide was rising fast and with it the tarpon were drifting toward the bays and coves and creeks.

I did not see another tail or break for three hours. Captain Thad kept poling along, into every likely nook he espied. R. C. and King had returned to the launch.

The day had grown still and warm, drowsy, with the breath and fragrance of summer. Birds, turtles, fish, were out of sight.

"Mebbe we'll find some up this cove," offered Thad, hopefully.

The water was clear and shallow, not more than three feet deep. Thad poled and paddled very cautiously along the overhanging banks of green.

"There goes one," he called, pointing to a swell on the surface. It traveled out into the cove. "Where there's one there's more."

Soon he pointed out a tarpon lying motionless half a foot under the surface, a long gleaming bar golden in hue through the amber water.

"He'll go less than a hundred," said Thad. "I believe I could make him take a bait. Shall I try or will we hunt for a big one?"

I was sorely tempted, but yielded to the suggestion in his last words. Then we glided slowly along, sometimes in the shade, but for the most part just outside the spreading foliage. It grew to be a fascinating game. I sighted several tarpon that Thad missed or did not point out. They did not move even a fin, though we passed so close I could

have touched them with an oar. Asleep! Thad assured
me this was the case, and I believed him.

We came to a narrow lane or rather opening in the
green bank. Two tarpon were lying on the surface, one
with fins out. They appeared to be moving very slightly.
Thad stuck his oar in the mud, and taking up my rod
he cast the bait right at the very nose of the big tarpon. I
watched with immense eagerness and curiosity. And just
what I had expected really happened. Roar! Smash!
Both tarpon plunged away from there, spreading huge
furrows and raising the mud.

"That fellow wasn't asleep," averred Thad. "He was
scared. But if he'd been asleep he'd taken the bait for a
mullet hopping close. An' he'd sure have hopped it."

"Well!" I ejaculated. "Then you must call this method
casting for tarpon?"

"Yes. An' it's the best way, at times like this."

We glided into the opening, to find it a small cove, shallow and quiet, where the wind could not ruffle the water.
The bottom appeared to be clean sand.

"I see a buster, over there," said Thad.

"I see one, over here," I replied.

"Yep. There's another in the middle—good big one,
too. All asleep! We'll sure hang one of these birds, as
R. C. says. Be careful not to make any noise."

Very slowly he moved the boat, in fact so slowly that
suspense wore on me. Yet I tingled with the pleasure of
the moment. Nor was it all because of the stalking of
big game! The little round cove was a beautiful place,
reposeful and absolutely silent, lonely, somehow dreamy.
A small blue heron flew away into a green aisle where the
water gleamed dark in shade.

Not for moments did I espy the big tarpon Thad was gliding so carefully toward. When I did see him I gasped. He lay close to the bottom in several feet of water. But I could see every detail of him. He shone brighter, a little more silvery gold than those we had seen out in the larger cove. His back looked black. I could scarcely believe this enormous shadow was really a fish, and a tarpon.

Thad halted about twenty-five feet distant, and with slow deliberation gently pushed his oar down into the sand. The boat had not made even a ripple.

"Now I'll hit him right on the nose," said Thad, with the utmost satisfaction.

He wound up the line until the leader was within a few inches of the tip; then he carefully balanced, and swung the bait.

"Watch. I'm bettin' he takes it," said Thad.

I was all eyes, and actually trembling. But only with the excitement of the place and the fish. I had not the remotest idea that the tarpon would do any more than wake up and lunge out of there.

Thad cast the bait. It hit with a plop and a splash, not right over the tarpon, but just in front of his nose. It certainly awoke him. I saw him jerk his fins. A little cloud of roily water rose from behind his tail.

Then, to my exceeding amaze, he moved lazily and began to elevate his body. It shone gold. It loomed up to turn silver. His tail came out and flapped on the surface. What a wonderful tail! It was a foot broad.

"He's got it," said Thad, handing the rod back to me.

"No!" I ejaculated, incredulously.

"Sure. I saw him take it in his mouth . . . So far so good. Now if he doesn't get leary!"

"Oh, he's moving off with it," I whispered, breathlessly. Indeed, that seemed the remarkable fact. The long, wide, shadowy shape glided away from the edge of the shade. I hoped it would move away from the boat. But he was going to pass close.

A triangular wave appeared on the water. It swelled. I heard the faint cut of my line as it swept out. I saw it move. My eyes were riveted on it. I pulled line off the reel and held my rod so it would run freely through the guides. What an impossible thing was happening! My heart felt swelling in my throat. I saw that great tarpon clearly in sunlit water not over three feet deep. I saw the checkerboard markings of his huge scales. I saw his lean, sharp, snub-nosed face and the immense black eye. All as he reached a point even with me!

Then he saw the boat, and no doubt Thad and me standing almost over him. Right before my rapt gaze he vanished. Next I heard a quick deep thrum. I saw a boiling cloud of muddy water rising toward the surface.

"He saw the boat!" yelled Thad. "He's scared. Soak him!"

But swift though I was, I could not throw on the drag, and reel in the slack line, and strike in time to avert a catastrophe. I seemed to freeze all over.

The very center of that placid cove upheaved in a flying maelstrom and there followed a roaring crash. A grand blazing fish leaped into the sunlight. He just cleared the water, so heavy was he, and seemed to hang for an instant in the air, a strange creature of the sea. Then the infinite grace and beauty of him underwent a change. His head suddenly became deformed. The wide gill-covers slapped open, exposing the red. He shook with such tremendous power and rapidity that he blurred in my sight. I saw the bait go flying far. He had thrown the hook.

With sounding smash he fell back. The water opened into a dark surging hole out of which flew muddy spray. With a solid, heavy thrum, almost like a roar of contending waters, the tarpon was gone. He left a furrowed wake that I shall never forget.

Slowly I reeled in, unmindful of the language of the usually mild Captain Thad. On the moment, as I recovered from what seemed a stunning check to my emotions, I did not feel the slightest pang. Instead, as the primitive thrills of the chase and capture, and the sudden paralyzing shock of fear and loss, passed away together, I experienced a perfect exhilaration.

Something wonderful had happened. I had seen something indescribably beautiful. Into my memory had been burned indelibly a picture of a sunlit, cloud-mirroring green-and-gold-bordered cove, above the center of which shone a glorious fish-creature in the air, wildly instinct with the action and daring of freedom.

Just then, before the exultation vanished, I felt as if I had been granted a marvelous privilege. Out of the inscrutable waters a beautiful fish had leaped, to show me fleetly the life and spirit of his element. And I had sought to kill!

When I laid my rod down and took my chair, motioning Captain Thad that we would go, I knew I had reached the end of this fishing trip. There is always an end to everything, even the longest lane. There is always a place for a story to end.

If I fished only to capture fish, my fishing trips would have ended long ago.

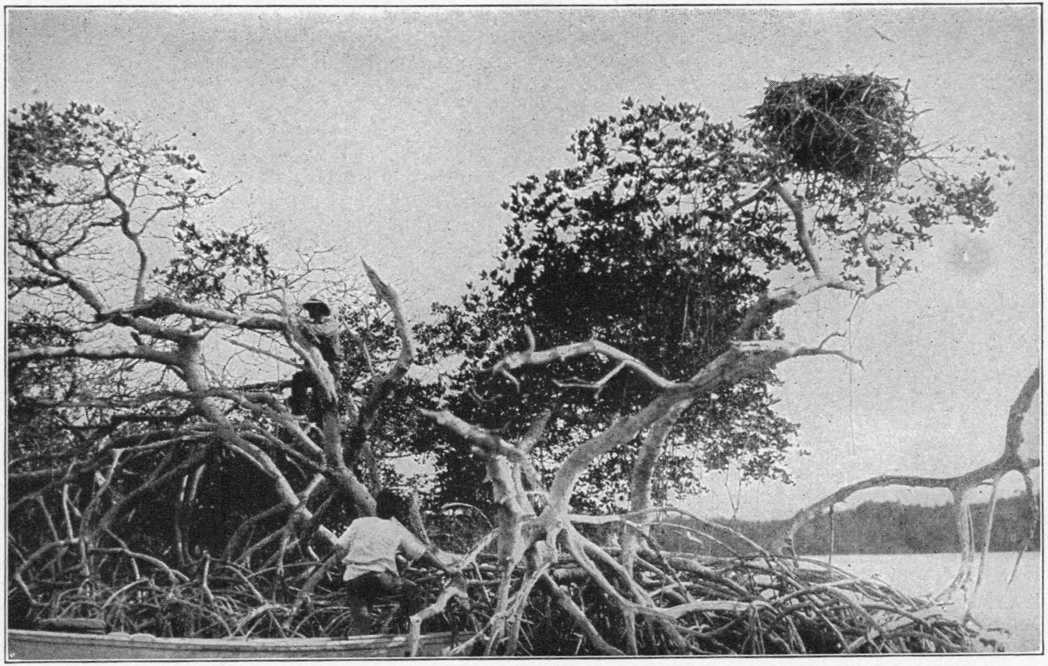

CLIMBING TO PHOTOGRAPH FISH-HAWK NEST

NOT ESPECIALLY WELCOMED BY YOUNG BIRDS

How the day had flown! The sun was westering, fading, from white to gold. A cloud pageant, different from any I had ever beheld, colored the western sky. Wild fowl were winging homeward flight into the heart of the sunset. A swamp blackbird caroled his deep-throated notes, sweet and plaintive, memorable of the north and boyhood days.

DOWN AN UNKNOWN JUNGLE RIVER

DOWN AN UNKNOWN JUNGLE RIVER

I

THE SANTA ROSA

TEN years ago I was going to Tampico for the tarpon fishing, and was traveling on the Mexican Central. For days I had looked out upon dusty drab desert, grotesque cactus plants, temples and cathedrals surmounting low rocky hills, and villages swarming with dark-skinned, sandal-footed natives. Beyond Cardenas, eight thousand feet above sea level, the desert was a barren waste of yucca and stone. Then we plunged off the plateau down the first of the great steps to the lowland. From the chill, bare region we descended winding canyons into a temperate zone, where all was green and fresh, and crossed a wide bench of farms and forests to the second step.

Then, from my window, I saw far below the gorgeous jungle of the tropics. I looked down upon the eternal summer. The train struck the down grade once more and I was lost in winding cuts and tunnels. Near the base of the towering mountain we came out upon the side of a deep canyon, where I caught a glimpse of Micas Falls. It was only a glimpse, but that was enough to pale the beauty of all the water-falls I had ever seen. The river burst from a notch between two heavily wooded slopes, and leaped out into the green void. The first fall was a white streak, ending in a dark pool; then came cascade after cas-

135

cade, fall after fall. Some were wide, others narrow, and
all white and green against the yellow rock. We curved
around the spur of the mountain, descended to the level,
to be lost in the luxuriance of the jungle growth. At a
little station called Valles we crossed the river. I had a
brief glance at the clear, green water, at the great cypress
trees, gray and graceful, with a long silvery waving moss,
at the tangled colorful banks. A water fowl, black as coal,
with white-crested wings, skimmed the water in swift, wild
flight, to disappear up the shady river lane.

The train sped on. But the beauty of Micas Falls and
the wildness of the jungle river remained with me. From
a native I learned that the river was called the Santa Rosa.
Where it went he did not know. That was a wild country.
The villages were few and were all along the line of the
railroad. It was then I conceived the idea of going down
the Santa Rosa in a canoe or boat. Where did that river
go? How many waterfalls and rapids hastened its journey
to the Gulf? What teeming life inhabited its rich banks?
How wild was the prospect! It haunted me!

That visit to Mexico was too full of a variety of interest and sport to permit of the Santa Rosa trip. The next
year I did not go South. For all that, I did not forget
the jungle river, and, as time passed, its call became more
insistent. Finally I returned to Tampico for the express
purpose of carrying out my cherished desire.

Tampico, during the winter months, was a rendezvous
for sportsmen from all over the world. By the middle of
February the broad Panuco River was dotted with boats
from Tamos to La Barra and everywhere the leaping Silver King cleaved the water in spectacular fight. I
watched tarpon jump till I was dazzled by the flash of

mother-of-pearl, and hung to a rod till my arms fell dead at my sides. Every few days I changed the rod for a gun; the shooting along the Panuco was as worth while as the fishing. An English globe-trotter with whom I hunted called it magnificent. From time to time I tried to interest some sportsman in my Santa Rosa trip. But I did not succeed very well, owing to the wonderful sport right at Tampico and the fact that I knew nothing at all about the Santa Rosa River.

Singularly, I seemed unable to gather any information. The *terra caliente,* or hot belt, along the curve of the Gulf was lined with streams, many of them unknown and unnamed. The broad Panuco swung round to the west and had its source somewhere up in the mountains. I concluded that the Santa Rosa was one of its headwaters. Valles lay up on the swell of the higher ground, some two thousand feet above sea-level, and was distant from Tampico about six hours by train. So, reckoning with the meandering character of jungle streams, I calculated that I would have approximately one hundred and seventy-five miles of travel by water from Valles to Tampico. There were Indian huts strung along the Panuco River, and fifty miles inland a village named Panuco. What lay between Valles and Panuco, down over the wild reaches of that jungle, I could only conjecture. But I was going to find out. That point once settled, I was easy in mind, though eager and restless to be off.

At the very outset of arranging practical details I encountered difficulties. It was necessary for me to have a companion, and a canoe or boat, and an outfit. After spending a whole day in vain endeavor to interest fishermen and hunters and Mexican *mozos* in my wild project, I

decided to outfit first and find a companion later. Of the
infinite variety of canoes in the waterways about Tampico
not one would suit my purpose. They had all been rough
hewn from solid tree trunks; they were long, slender,
graceful, pretty to look at and easy to handle on the shallow lagoons, but they were too heavy and cumbersome for
fast water. Failing to find a canoe, I began to look about
for a suitable flat-bottom boat, one of light, strong build.
Of the hundreds of fishing boats along the Panuco not one
would serve. I had handled boats in swift rapids and I
knew what I wanted. Happening to think of Micas Falls
just then, I had a momentary chill and a check to enthusiasm. What if I encountered, in coming down the Santa
Rosa, some such series of cascades as those which made
Micas Falls.

I had almost decided to have a suitable boat built, when
I chanced to make the acquaintance of a young American
named George Allen. He was a slim, keen-eyed youth,
probably more of a boy in age than he looked or pretended.
He had spent a couple of years in Tampico, working in railroad offices, and had just begun a much longed-for vaca-
tion. I told him what I was hunting for in the way of a
boat, and he replied that he knew just where to get it. He
led me down narrow lanes, between the painted stone houses
with brown-tiled roofs and iron-barred windows, till we
reached the canal. We entered a yard where buzzards,
goats, and red razor-back pigs were contesting for scaven-
ger rights. Allen took me into a boathouse and pointed
out a long, light skiff with a flat bottom. I did not need
the importunities of the boatkeeper to make me eager about
this particular boat. I jumped in, shoved it out, rowed up
the canal, pulled and turned, backed water, and whistled my

YOUNG FISH HAWKS, BUT FULL GROWN AND VERY TAME

THE RETURN OF THE MOTHER FISH HAWK. TIME TO GET DOWN!

delight. For my purpose the boat was perfect and I made a deal with the man for one peso a day.

Young Allen expressed his curiosity, and I told him of my Santa Rosa trip and that I must now find a comrade.

"Take me along," he said, promptly.

There was a note of American spirit in his voice, a flash and a laugh in his keen eyes, that made me take him up at once. We bought a long strip of canvas, nine feet wide, blankets, cooking utensils, and supplies for three weeks. Then we set out to get a boatman. All of the *mozos* we interviewed were anxious to work, but when acquainted with the nature of the trip they refused point-blank.

"*Tigre!*" exclaimed one.

"*Javelin!*" said another.

The big spotted jaguar of the jungle and the wild boar, or peccary, were held in much dread by the natives.

Finally I met a *mozo* named Pepe, who had rowed a boat for me two years before. He looked sadly in need of a job, still he did not ask for it. Allen told me that Pepe had been one of the best boatmen on the river until *cañu,* the fiery white liquor to which the natives are addicted, had ruined his reputation. Pepe wore an old sombrero, a cotton shirt and sash, and ragged trousers. He was barefooted. I noted the set of his muscular neck, his brawny shoulders and arms, and appreciated the years of rowing that had developed them. But Pepe's haggard face, deadened eyes, and listless manner made me doubt his efficiency for an adventure like mine. Still, there never is any telling what a man can do. Pepe's hopeless dejection excited my sympathy. So I clapped him on the shoulder and asked him if he would like to work for several weeks at three pesos a day. That was treble the *mozo's* price. Pepe nearly fell off the railing of the canal bridge, where I had found him sitting, and a light flashed into his face as warm and bright as sunshine. He began to jabber, "Si señor," and to wave his nervous brown hands. I suspected that Pepe needed a job as badly as anything. I knew it when I caught a word here and there about wife and children. On the spot I conceived a liking for Pepe and believed I could trust him. Besides, in hiring guides or choosing companions for a wild adventure, I had learned to trust to an inexplicable impulse. I thought I knew how to deal with poor, unhappy Pepe. So I gave him money, told him to buy a change of clothes and a pair of shoes, and to come to my hotel the next day.

"He'll spend the money for *cañu* and not show up to-morrow," said Allen.

My American acquaintances in Tampico, particularly the genial proprietor of the hotel, had much to say about my wild-goose chase. At first they could not take me seriously. Then they mingled astonishment with amusement and concern. They advised me not to go; they declared they would not let me go. There were the ticks, the bats, the tigers, the boars, the alligators, the snakes, not to mention fevers, swamps, sand bars, bogs, and a river that nobody ever had explored. My friend, the hotel man, expressed himself freely:

"It's a fool trip. What's the sense in going way up there? You don't know where you'll come out. The river here is full of tarpon now; there are millions of ducks and geese on the lagoons; you can kill deer and turkey right on the edge of town. If you want *tigre* and *javelin* go out to one of the ranches where they have dogs to hunt with, where you've a chance for your life. These tigers and boars will kill a man. There's all the sport any one wants right close. It's not safe, especially with a boy and that *mozo* Pepe. He's soaked with *cañu* and he's crazy. He'll stick a knife in you or run off and leave you when you most need help. It's a wild trip. Don't go!"

Of course, my genial friend's remarks made me only the more eager to be on the way to the Santa Rosa.

"Well, if you must go, there's one thing I want you to find out," he concluded. "We've always wondered how far the tarpon run up the Panuco. Nobody knows. It's a mooted question."

When it came to getting the boat shipped we met with more obstacles. But for the friendly offices of a Texan, an employee of the railroad, we never could have convinced the shipping agent that a boat was merchandise. The Texan said he would arrange it and got me a freight bill. He took an entirely different view of my enterprise from that of the hotel man, and in the cool, curt speech of a ranger, he said:

"You'll have the greatest time of your life. I worked at the Valles station as operator for a year. That jungle is full of game. I killed three tigers while I was there. You want to look out for those big yellow fellows. They make for a man the moment they see him. You just have to shoot. Then the pigs, they are bad. They put me up a tree more than once. I don't know anything about the Santa Rosa and never heard where it goes. There are no boats or canoes at Valles. The stream is full of rapids, and alligators, too, don't forget that. You've sure got sport coming to you."

Pepe presented himself at the hotel next day an entirely

different person. He was clean-shaven and no longer disheveled. He wore a new sombrero, a white cotton shirt, a red sash, and blue trousers. He carried a small bundle, a pair of shoes, and a long machete. The dignity with which he approached before all the other *mozos* was not lost upon me. A sharp scrutiny satisfied me that Pepe had not been drinking. I gave him several errands to do and then set him to packing my effects. These I ordered taken to the station in the afternoon in his charge.

Our train was to leave at five, and Allen and I went down early. It was the time when the *mozos* were returning from the day's tarpon fishing on the river, and they, with the *cargodores,* streamed to and fro on the platform. Pepe was there, keeping guard over our outfit. He had lost his fame among his old associates, either justly or unjustly, and for long had been an outsider, considered as worthless. Here he was in charge of a pile of fine guns, fishing tackle, grips, and supplies—a collection representing a fortune to him and his simple class. He had been trusted with it. It was under his eye. All his old associates passed by to see him there. That was a great hour for Pepe. What a little thing will win back a man's hope and self-respect! Pepe looked bright, alert, and supremely happy. It would have fared ill with loafers or sneak thieves had they made themselves free with any of the articles under his watchful eye.

We left Tampico at five o'clock. The broad Panuco was rippling with the incoming tide. Wild fowl dotted its green bosom. Here and there splashes and spurts showed where playful *savalo* were breaking water. Great greenbacked tarpon rolled their silver sides against the little waves. White cranes and blue herons stood like statues upon the reedy bars. Low down over the opposite bank of the river a long line of wild geese winged its way toward a distinct shimmering lagoon. And against the gold and crimson of the sunset sky a flight of wild ducks stood out in bold black relief. We crossed the Tamesi River and began to draw away from the Panuco. On the left, wide marshes, gleaming purple in the darkening light, led the eye far beyond to endless pale lagoons. Birds of many kinds skimmed the weedy flats. Here was a flock of egrets, the beautiful white fowl with the priceless plumes. There was a string of pink flamingoes, tall, grotesque, wading along with waddling stride, feeding with heads underwater.

At Tamos, twelve miles out of Tampico, we entered the jungle. Thereafter I could see nothing but the impenetrable green walls that lined the track. We reached Las Palmas at dark and then began to ascend the first step of the mountain. It was a steep grade, and we climbed perhaps two thousand feet. The moon was in its first quarter. In the tropics the moon is large, radiant, a wonderful green-gold. It shed a soft luminous glow down upon the sleeping, tangled web of jungle. The land was new and strange to me, so vastly different from barren desert or iron-ribbed mountain canyon, and it thrilled me with nameless charm.

About ten o'clock we arrived at Valles. A crowd of chattering natives, with wide-peaked sombreroes and blankets over their shoulders, crowded round the little stone station. Visitors were rare in that village, as was manifested by our difficulty in securing lodging for the night. We had about decided to camp on the station platform when Pepe found a place where we could sleep. We were led into a big ramshackle house. There were no lights, and we bumped into things while following our guide. Finally we climbed to a kind of loft, where the moonlight streamed in at the open sides. Our beds were cots made of heavy canvas, stretched over a high framework. Mine was as high as my head and most awkward to climb into. I was of half a mind to sleep on the floor, but, feeling ashamed of so poor a courage at the outset of a dangerous trip, I swung myself up and by dint of muscular effort managed to get into the cot. My comrades were not so lucky at first. Pepe's cot collapsed, and Allen, in climbing up, swung over too hard and rolled off the other side. The thump he made when he dropped jarred the whole loft. The way Pepe laughed at this mishap and the way Allen went to climbing up the framework of his trestle bed pleased me exceedingly. For a sense of humor and a good fighting spirit are valuable attributes in a hunter's party.

When I awakened the sun was shining through holes in the thatched roof. We descended from our lofty beds without breaking any bones, had an early breakfast, and were ready for the day. Valles consisted of a few stone and wood houses along a main street and a number of huts made of poles and thatched roofs of palm leaves. The inhabitants manifested a kindly interest in us, which changed to consternation when they saw the boat and learned of our project. Pepe questioned every native we met, and all he could learn about the Santa Rosa was that we would never get beyond a rapid several kilometres below Valles. There were a few fields under cultivation around the village, and beyond rose the impenetrable jungle. It seemed useless to try to find out anything about the river. We did not run across a man who had ever heard of the headwaters of the Panuco. But they told us enough about tigre and javelin to make Pepe turn pale and Allen's hair stand on end and to give me a thrill and a shock both in one.

The hardest task, so far, developed in the matter of transporting boat and supplies to the river. At first we were informed that there was no wagon, and then that there was no road. We tried to hire a handcar so as to move the outfit along the railroad track to the bridge, but it was impossible. Pepe came to our aid again with a native who had a cart. This fellow said he knew a trail that went to a point from which it would be easy to carry the boat to the river. His cart was a remarkable vehicle. It consisted of a narrow body between enormously high wheels, and a trio of tired little mules was hitched to it. The driver at first willingly agreed to haul our outfit for one peso, but when he drove up to the station, to be surrounded by neighbors and friends, he suddenly discovered that he could not possibly accommodate us. Patiently we endeavored to persuade him. No, it was not possible. He made no excuses, but he looked mysterious. When I came out bluntly and offered him five pesos he began to sweat. From the look of his eyes I judged he had not earned five pesos in five months. But his cunning kept him from weakening. He had the only cart in the village and fortune seemed hovering over him. He refused my offer.

I had dealt with his kind many times before.

"Ten pesos!"

He began to jabber like a crazy man. We lifted the boat upon the cart and tied it fast, then packed the rest of the outfit inside. I was surprised to see how easily the little mules started off with such a load. At the edge of the jungle I looked back toward the station. The motley crowd of natives was watching us, making excited gestures

and shouting. Our guide drove into a narrow trail, which
closed behind him. We followed on foot, brushing aside
the bushes. I drew a breath of relief as I got into the
shade. It was about noon of March 2nd, and very hot.
The trail was lined and overgrown with slender trees, standing very close, making dense shade. Many birds, some of
beautiful coloring, flitted in the branches. In about an
hour we came to a little clearing where there were several
thatched huts. I heard the puffing of an engine, and looking out through the trees to see the railroad, I realized we
had reached the pumping station and the bridge.

Our driver rounded up six natives, who lifted the boat
upon their shoulders. As they were carrying it down the
trail they encountered two Mexicans who had never seen
a boat.

"What is it, the devil?" they ejaculated.

If I needed any more than had already been said about
the wildness of the Santa Rosa, I had it in the bewilder-
ment of these natives. A beautiful wild river, to which
boats were unknown! When I conceived the idea of the
trip I had not hoped for so much.

There was a deep satisfaction in the moment. As I followed the men down the trail there was little I failed to
note. I heard the soft rush of water over stones, and the
mourning of turtledoves. We rounded a little hill to come
abruptly upon the dense green mass of river foliage. Giant
cypress trees, bearded with gray moss, fringed the banks.
Through the dark rich green of leaves I caught sight of
light green water. Birds rose all about me; there was the
whir of ducks and rustling in the thick underbrush. We
penetrated the dark shade and came out into the open on a
grassy point bordered with rocks.

ZANE GREY IN THE MANGROVES

THE FORBIDDING AND TERRIBLE MANGROVE FOREST

The Santa Rosa, glistening, green, swift, murmured at my feet. The men dropped the boat into the water and went back for the rest of the outfit. I looked up the shady lane of the river, and thought of the moment three years before when I had crossed the bridge on the train. How strange it was, at that moment, to see a large black duck with white-crested wings sweep by swift as the wind! I had seen that wild fowl, or one of his kind, three years before, and he had haunted my dreams.

It took me only a moment to decide to make camp there, and the next day to try to reach Micas Falls. The mountains seemed so close at hand, and were so high that, early as it was, the western sun hung over the blue summits. The notch where the Santa Rosa cut through the range stood out clear. At the most it was not more than eighteen miles. So I planned to spend a day or so pulling up the river and then to turn for the downstream trip.

Pepe took his long machete into the brush to cut firewood. Young Allen and I put up the strip of canvas. We stretched a rope between two trees, threw the canvas over it, and pegged down the ends. I regretted that we had no tent, but as such a thing could not be bought in Tampico, we had to take what we could get.

"I'm going to sleep between you and Pepe," Allen said. "If we don't have some hot old times keeping things out of this tent I'll miss my guess."

"I dare say we won't be able to keep things out," I replied, dubiously.

Just as Pepe came into the camp, staggering under a load of wood, a flock of russet-colored ducks swung around the bend below. They alighted near the shore opposite us and about sixty yards distant. George made a dive into the outfit for one of his guns. Coming out with a 22-caliber, he loaded quickly and fired into the flock. He crippled one; the others flew away. Then he began to waste shells trying to kill the duck. Pepe jumped into the boat and with a long stick poled out into a shallow rift. The duck floated into the current and went round the bend, with Pepe in pursuit and Allen yelling along the shore. When they returned a little later they had the duck, which was one of a variety unknown to me. Pepe had fallen overboard and George was wet to his knees. Both were glowing with enthusiasm. I began to feel I had not made a mistake in my choice of companions.

About the middle of the afternoon the heat was intense. I found myself favoring the shade, and noted that George and Pepe did likewise. During this hot spell, which lasted from three to five, there was a quiet, and a lack of life about the camp that surprised me. It was a sleeping stillness; even the insects seemed drowsy. Not a duck, and scarcely a bird, passed by. I heard the mourning of a turtledove and was at once struck with the singular deep, full tone. Several times the trains crossed the bridge and at intervals the engine at the pumping tank puffed and chugged. From time to time natives walked out on the bridge to stare long and curiously at us.

When the sun set behind the mountain a hard breeze swooped down the river. I did not know what to make of it, and at first thought we were in for a storm. But Pepe said that the wind blew that way every day. For a while it tossed the willows and waved the Spaniard's beard upon the cypresses. Then as suddenly as it had come it died away, taking the heat with it.

Whereupon we began to get supper. The river water

was cold and clean, but I decided to boil all that we used. This matter of water had bothered me more than anything in consideration of the trip, and I felt relieved to find it apparently safe. While Pepe and I busied ourselves about the camp fire, George sat on a rock watching the wild fowl flying upstream. Once he yelled: "Canvas-backs!" We had supper, finding the russet duck much to our taste. I made a mental note of Pepe's capacity and was glad there appeared to be prospects of plenty of meat. While we were eating, a group of natives gathered upon the bridge to watch us. I would not have liked to intercept their opinion of us from their actions.

Then night came on almost before we were ready for it. I got out the mosquito netting, but to my amazement it was not needed. We lay down under our open-sided tent and were soon fast asleep. I awoke a couple of times during the night and rolled over to find a softer spot on the hard bed. These times I was aware only of the incessant hum of insects. But when I opened my eyes to the gray morning light I heard something that made me sit up with a jump. It was a deep booming sound, different from anything with which I was familiar. I awakened Pepe.

"Listen."

In a little while the heavy "boo-oom! . . . boo-oom!" came to us again. There was a resemblance to the first strong beats of a drumming grouse, only that this sound was infinitely wilder.

Pepe called it something like "Faisen Real."

This was as new to me as the noise itself. Pepe explained it was made by a huge black bird, not unlike a turkey. It had a golden plume and could run as fast as a deer. I conceived a desire to see such a strange bird, so I got up. The sound was not repeated. Almost immediately, however, the thicket across the river awoke to another sound, as much a contrast to the boom as could have been imagined. It was a bird medley. At first I thought of magpies, then parrots, but Pepe solved the riddle with another word hard to spell.

"Chicalocki," he said.

And that seemed just like what they were singing. It was a sharp, clear song: "Chic-a-lock-i . . . chic-a-lock-i," and to judge from the full chorus there must have been many birds.

"They're a kind of pheasant," added George, "and make dandy pot-stews."

The chicalocki ceased their salute to the morning; and then as the river mist melted away under the rising sun, other birds took it up. Notes new to me burst upon the air. Familiar old songs thrilled me—the sweet carol of the meadow lark, the whistle of the quail, the mellow call of the swamp blackbird. The songs blended in an exquisite harmony.

"Wait," said Pepe, with a laugh.

I did not know what to wait for, but I was enjoying the moment and anticipating much. Ducks began to whir by; blackbirds alighted in the trees across the river. Suddenly I was astounded at a great discordant screeching and the sweeping rush of myriads of wings. I looked up to see the biggest flock of birds I had ever seen.

"Parrots!" I yelled.

Indeed they were, and they let me know it. They flew across the river, wheeled to come back, all the time screeching, and then they swept into the tops of the cypress trees.

A TUNNEL IN THE DARK MANGROVES

WALKING ON THE STIFF IRON-LIKE ROOTS

AT LOW TIDE

SHOWING THE WEB OF MANGROVE ROOTS

"Red-heads," said Allen, in disgust. "Wait until you see the yellow-heads."

The red-heads were quite sufficient for me at the moment. They broke into a chattering, screaming, cackling discordance. It was plainly directed at us. These intelligent birds were curious and resentful. They were scolding us, as Pepe put it. I sat there for half an hour, while he and George got breakfast, and reveled in the din. That morning serenade, for so I took it, was worth the trip.

Presently the parrots flew away, and I was surprised to learn that most of the other birds had ceased singing. They had set about the business of the day, something it was high time for me to consider. Breakfast over, we broke camp. Packing the outfit in the boat was a problem for me. It had to be packed for a trip with many things taken into consideration. Balance was all-important; a flat surface easy to crawl and jump over was absolutely necessary; comfort was not to be overlooked. I placed a small bucket of preserved mullet, some bottles of kerosene and *cañu,* and a lantern up close to the bow. Then I cut out the first bow seat. I had brought a small steamer trunk, and this, full of supplies, we put in next. The two flat boxes with the rest of the supplies filled up the space between the trunk and the rowing seat. By slipping an extra pair of oars, coils of rope, the ax, and a few other articles between the gunwales and the trunk and the boxes we made them fit snugly and tightly. We cut off a piece of the heavy canvas, and folding it narrow, laid it lengthwise with the blankets over the top. This made a level surface, one that could be gotten over quickly, or a place to sleep, for that matter, and effectually disposed of the bow half of the boat. The grips in which we carried clothing we put under the second seat. I arranged the other piece of canvas in the stern so that it projected up at the back of the seat. I was thinking of the waves we would buffet in going stern first downstream through the rapids. The fishing tackle and guns we laid flat from seat to seat. Last of all we placed the ammunition on one side of the gunwale and my grip with my camera, films, medicines, etc., on the other. I was delighted to find the boat trim and more buoyant, with our additional weight, than I had dared to hope. Pepe took the oars and we started upstream.

Soon the iron structure of the bridge disappeared as we turned a bend. I had expected a long shady ride, but shallow water and gravelly rapids made us get out to wade and pull the boat. It was not such hard work at first. We were fresh and eager, and hauled the heavy boat up swift and shallow channels, making as good time as if we were rowing in smooth water. Then as the sun began to grow hot the wading and splashing was pleasant. We passed little islands green with willows and came to high clay banks gradually wearing away, and then met with rocky restrictions in the stream bed. From around the bend a hollow roar, deeper than the others, told us of a fall. We found it a swift rushing incline, very narrow and deep, so that we had to work hard in pulling the boat along the margin.

Above this fall the water was deep and still. We got in the boat and turned a curve to enter a long, beautiful stretch of river. The green shady lane was alive with birds and water fowl. Ducks of various kind rose before us. There were white, blue, gray and speckled herons, some standing six feet tall. Then there were many varieties of bitterns, one with a purple back and a white breast. They were very tame and sat on the overhanging branches, uttering dismal croaks. Everywhere were the flash and glitter and moving gleam of birds in flight, up and down and across the river. George began to pop away with his .22-caliber, and as he appeared to be doing little harm I made no objection.

The strangeness, beauty, and life of this jungle stream absorbed me. I did not take my guns from their cases. The water was bright green and very deep; here and there were the swirls of playing fish. The banks were high and densely covered with luxuriant foliage. Huge cypress trees, moss covered, leaned half-way across the river. Giant gray-barked cebias spread long branches thickly tufted with aloes, orchids, and other jungle parasites. Palm trees lifted slender stems and graceful broad-leaved heads. Clumps of bamboo thrust an enormous green arch out over the banks. These bamboo trees were particularly beautiful to me. A hundred yellow black-circled stems grew out of the ground close together, and as they rose high they gracefully leaned their bodies and drooped their tips. The leaves were arrowy, exquisite in their fineness.

I looked up the long river lane, bright in the sun, dark and still under the moss-veiled cypresses, at the turning vines and blossoming creepers, at the changeful web of moving birds, and I indulged to the fullest that haunting sense of wild places.

"Chicalocki," said Pepe, suddenly.

A flock of long-tailed birds, resembling the pheasant in body, were sailing across the river. Again George made a dive for the gun. This was a sixteen-gauge and worn out. He shot twice at the birds on the wing. Then Pepe rowed under the overhanging branches and George killed three chicalocki with his rifle. They were olive green in color and the tail had a brownish cast. They were plump and promised fine eating.

"Pato real!" yelled Pepe, pointing excitedly up the river.

Several black fowl, as large as geese, hove in sight, flying pretty low. I caught a glimpse of wide white-crested wings, and knew then that these were the birds I had thought of for so long.

"Load up and get ready," I said to George. "They're coming fast. Shoot ahead of them."

What swift, powerful flyers these birds were! They swooped up as they sighted the boat and afforded a splendid target. Allen's little sixteen-gauge rang out. I heard the shot strike. The leader stopped in midair, dipped, and plunged with a sounding splash. We picked him up and found him to be most beautiful and as large and heavy as a goose. His black feathers shone with the luster of an opal, and the pure white of the shoulder of the wings made a remarkable contrast.

"George, we have enough meat for to-day, more than we can use. Don't shoot any more," I said.

He appeared to be disappointed, but laid aside the gun without any comment.

Pepe resumed rowing, and I told him to keep under the overhanging branches and to row without splashing. He was skillful with the oars, so that we glided along silently. How we were rewarded for this stealth! Birds of rare and brilliant plumage flitted among the leaves. There was one, a long slender bird, gold and black, with a white ring about his neck. There were little yellow-breasted king-fishers no bigger than a wren, and great red-breasted king-fishers with blue backs and tufted heads. We passed under a leaning cebia that was covered with orchids. I saw the slim, sharp head of a snake dart from among the leaves. His neck was as big as my wrist. For a moment I fingered the trigger of George's gun, then decided not to kill him. There would be plenty of time for me to shoot, besides I did not care to disturb the silence. The snake reminded me, however, that the hunters had told me of snakes in this jungle which measured from fifteen to twenty feet, and were as large as a man's leg.

Most of the way the bank was too high and steep and overgrown for any animal to get down to the water, still there were dry gullies, or arroyos, every few hundred yards, and these showed the tracks of many beasts. Often we would hear a pattering of hard feet, but we would reach one of these drinking places only to see a little cloud of dust. So I cautioned Pepe to row slower and nearer in to the bank. Then we came abruptly into a band of racoons, not less than thirty-five, big and little, all with long white-ringed tails. What a scampering they set up! A very small one, too young to be much afraid or move quickly, just managed to evade Pepe's brown hand as he leaned from the boat.

So we glided upstream. Often I motioned Pepe to stop in dark cool places under the golden green canopy of bam-boos. We could hear the fluttering of birds in the thick jungle, rustlings and soft, stealthy steps. Then as we moved on, George would whisper and point to some brown or black animal vanishing in the thicket. Three times I caught sight of a gray spotted form slipping away into the shade, and the last time I directed Pepe's eye quickly enough. "Tiger-cat," he said. This I knew was not the jaguar, the great spotted lord of the jungle, but all the same I took up Allen's .32-caliber and tried to find a way up the bank. There was no place to climb up, unless I tried the branches of trees and drooping bamboos. In fact, there were only here and there low stretches where we could see over the matted roots and creepers. Then as we continued up the river the sound of the rapids put hunting out of my mind. We had Micas Falls to reach.

That long stretch of deep river ended in a wide, shallow, noisy rapid. Fir trees lined the banks. The palms, cypresses, bamboos, and the flowery mossy growths were not here in evidence. Thickly wooded hills rose on each side. The jungle looked sear and yellow. Before we had reached the top of that rapids we stumbled upon an eight-foot alligator. Pepe hit it with an oar. Thereafter we waded carefully in the shallow water.

Above the rapids extended a quarter-mile stretch where we could row, and then came another long rapid. When we had waded up that one it was only to come to another. It began to be hard work. But I kept the boys buckled down and we made good time. We pulled up seventeen or eighteen rapids and covered distance that I estimated to be about ten miles. The blue mountains loomed closer and higher, but I began to have doubts of getting to Micas Falls that day.

Moreover, the falls grew rougher as we ascended the stream. Finally we came to one that had long rung in my ears. All the water of the river rushed down on the right-hand side in a channel scarcely twenty feet wide. It was deep and swift. With the aid of ropes and by much hard wading and pulling we at last got the boat up.

A little farther on was another bothersome rapid. At length we came to a series of falls, steps in the river, that barred our progress. I climbed up on the bank here to find the country open, with patches of jungle, groves of palms, and wide flats leading to the hills. The mountains were close and I caught a glimpse of Micas Falls. We might have reached the falls by extraordinary exertions, but in view of the long trip down the river it was not to be thought of. Besides, I saw stock fences across the river and heard a train rumbling up on the mountain slope, and concluded we were near one of the native villages along the railroad.

We made camp on a grassy bench above a foam-flecked pool. I left the boys to get things into shape for supper, and taking my camera, hurried off to try to get a picture of Micas Falls. I found open places and bypaths through the dry, brushy forest. I saw evidences of forest fire and then knew what had ruined that part of the jungle. There were no birds. It was farther than I had estimated to the base of the foothill I had marked, but, loath to give up, I hung on and finally reached a steep, scaly, thorny ascent. Going up I nearly suffocated with the heat. Ample reward, however, there was for my exertions. Micas Falls glistened in the distance like a string of green fans connected by silver ribbons. I remained there watching it while the sun set in the golden notch between the mountains.

On the way down, as I waded through a flat overgrown with coarse grass and bushes, I jumped a herd of deer, eight in number. These small, sleek gray animals appeared tame, yet I could not photograph them. It cost me a little effort to decide not to take my rifle, but as we already had meat there was nothing to do except to let the deer go. When I got back to camp Pepe grinned at me, and pointing to little red specks upon my shirt, he said, "Pinilius."

"Aha! the ticks," I exclaimed.

They were exceedingly small, not to be seen without close scrutiny. They could not be brushed off, so laboriously I had to pick them off. Allen and Pepe laughed at me, and to my surprise seemed to derive some sort of satisfaction from the incident.

"Say! these ticks don't bother me any."

Pepe grunted and George called out:

"Just wait until you get the big fellows—the garrapatoes."

It developed presently that the grass and bushes on our camp site contained millions of both pinilius and garrapatoes. I found several of the larger ticks—they were almost the size of my little finger nail, crawling upon me, but I was not bitten. Pepe and George, however, had no such luck, as was manifested by exclamations at different times. By the time they had cut down the few bushes and carried in a stock of firewood both were covered by the little pests. Whereupon they sat down and became engaged in a task infinitely puzzling to me. Both Pepe and George were cigarette smokers, and I saw them burning the ticks off shirt sleeves and trousers legs. But this was not the feat that puzzled me. It was when they held the red point of their cigarettes close to their naked flesh. I grew over-curious and had to see that performance at close range. They were as sober as judges.

"What in the deuce do you do that for?"

"Popping ticks," replied George.

The fact of the matter was soon clear to me. The ticks stuck on as if glued. When the hot end of the burning cigarette was held within a quarter of an inch of them, they simply blew up, exploded with a pop. I could distinguish plainly between the tiny pop of the pinilius exploding and the heavy pop of a garrapato.

"But, boy, while you are taking time to do that, a half dozen other ticks can bite you!" I exclaimed.

"Sure they can," replied George, "but if they get on me I'll kill 'em. I don't mind the little ones—it's the garrapatoes I hate!"

On the other hand, Pepe minded most the pinilius. I took my exploding in laughter.

"Boys, from now on you're Pinilius Pepe and Garrapato George."

"You'll laugh on the other side of your face soon," replied George. "In three days you will be popping ticks yourself."

The prospect did look serious to me. When I found the grass under our canvas alive with the insects I began to cast about in my mind for a remedy. On the ridge above the bench was a palm tree and under it were many dead leaves. They were enormous in size, had long stems, and were as dry as tinder. I hit upon the idea of setting fire to these leaves and dragging them about over the grass. When lighted they made a flaming hot torch. It did not take long to scorch all the ticks near that camp.

Then we had supper and enjoyed it hugely. The scene went well with the camp fire and game dinner. There were the foamy pool, the brawling rapids, the tufted palm trees, and above the dark blue mountain. We went to bed at dusk and were so tired that we dropped into slumber at once.

In the night a yell awakened me. I sat up, clutching my revolver. The white moonlight made everything as clear as day. George raised himself, stupid with sleep. But Pepe was not under the canvas. I heard him thrashing about outside. Leaping up, I ran to him and found him beating and clawing and tearing at himself like one suddenly possessed. I though he had been stung by something or bitten by a snake.

"Pepe, what is it?" I shouted.

"Look! Look!" he cried, pointing downward. Then he yelled an unintelligible Spanish word.

I saw a stream of black ants pouring over the ground. It was an army of jungle ants on a march! They made a straight line across the bench, and their passage had led under the canvas. As Pepe happened to be in that line they surged over him, and as he had awakened and moved they promptly bit him.

The stream of ants was about a foot wide and black as coal. It moved steadily, with order, and quite rapidly, and took a full hour to pass through our open tent.

"What did I tell you?" asked George, sleepily, as we turned in again. "It's coming to us!"

II

DOWNSTREAM

WE slept well the remainder of the night, and owing to the break in our slumbers, did not awaken early. The sun shone hot when I rolled out; a creamy mist was dissolving over the curve of the mountain range; parrots were screeching in the near-by trees.

After breakfast we broke camp and packed the boat. Before departing I carefully looked over the ground to see that nothing was left, and espied a fish line which George had baited and set the night before. I told him to pull it up. I happened to be busy at the boat when George started to take in the line. An exclamation from Pepe, George's yell, then a tremendous splash made me jump up on the bank in double-quick time.

George was staggering along, leaning back hard on the heavy fish line. A long swirl in the water told of a powerful fish. It was pulling George in.

"Let go the line!" I yelled.

But instead of complying the boy yelled for Pepe, and went clear to his knees before Pepe got to him. Both then hauled on the line. There was another tremendous splash, and the line slackened. The fish had torn loose. I examined the big tarpon hook and found it bent out of shape —the first time I had even seen one bent. George said he had baited the set line with half a pound of duck meat. Pepe could not name the fish, or whatever it was, and I certainly had no idea.

"I've held big tarpon," said George, "but this fish was pulling me in."

"I wish we could stay to have another try at him," I replied. "But we must be on the move—we don't know what we have before us."

When we got into the boat I took the oars, much to Pepe's surprise. It was necessary to explain to him that I would handle the boat in swift water. We shoved off, and I sent one regretful glance up the river, at the shady

aisle between the green banks, at the white rapids, and
the great colored dome of the mountain. I almost hesitated
with the desire to see more of that jungle covered mountain, but something told me to lose no time in the trip
down the Santa Rosa. There did not seem to be any reason
for hurry, yet I felt that it was necessary.

Going downstream on any river, mostly, is pleasure, but
drifting on the swift current of the Santa Rosa and rowing
under the wonderful moss-bearded cypresses was almost
like a dream. It was too beautiful to seem real. The
smooth stretch before the first rapid was short, however,
and all my attention had to be given to the handling of the
boat. I saw that George and Pepe both expected to get
out and wade down the falls as we had waded up. I had a
surprise in store for them. The rapids that we could not
shoot would have to be pretty bad.

"You're getting close," shouted George, warningly.

With two sweeps of the oars I turned the boat stern first
downstream; we dipped on the low green incline, and
sailed down toward the waves. We bunted with a shock
into the first wave and the water flew all over the boys.
Pepe was tremendously excited; he yelled and made wild
motions with his hands; George looked a little frightened.
Whatever the rapids appeared to them, it was magnificent
to me, and it was play to manage the boat in such water.
A little pull on one oar, and then on the other kept the
stern straight downstream. The channel I could make out
a long way ahead. I amused myself by watching George
and Pepe. There were rocks in the channel and the water
rose angrily about them. A glance was enough to assure
me that we could float over these without striking. But
the boys thought we were going to hit every stone and

were uneasy all the time. Twice I had to work to pass ledges and sunken trees upon which the current bore down hard. When we neared one of these I dipped the oars and pulled back to stop or lessen the momentum, then a stroke turned the boat half broadside to the current. That would force us to one side, and another stroke would set the boat straight. At the bottom of this rapids we encountered a long triangle of choppy waves over which we bumped and splashed. We came through with nothing wet except the raised flap of canvas in the stern. Pepe regarded me with admiring eyes; said I would make a *"grande mozo"* and George proclaimed shooting rapids great sport.

We drifted through several little rifts and then stopped at the head of the narrow chute that had been such a stumbling block to us on the way up. Surveyed from above, this long narrow channel, with several S curves, was a fascinating bit of water for a canoeist. It tempted me to shoot it even with the boat. But I remembered the four-foot waves at the bottom, and besides I resented the importunity of that spirit of daring so early in the game. Risk and perhaps peril would come soon enough. So I decided to walk along the shore and float the boat through with a rope.

The thing looked a good deal easier than it turned out to be. We got halfway through without any trouble, then at the narrowest point and most abrupt curve Pepe misunderstood me and pulled back on the rope when he should have let it slack. The boat swung in, nearly smashing me against the bank, and the sweeping current began to bulge dangerously near the gunwale. I saw disaster and yelled for Pepe to let go. Instead he pulled all the harder. To cap the climax, George, who was trying to get the rope out of Pepe's muscular hands, suddenly dropped it and made a dive for his rifle.

"Deer! deer!" he cried, hurriedly throwing a shell into the chamber. He shot downstream, and, looking that way, I saw several deer under the firs on the rocky flat. George shot three more times and the bullets went spinging into the trees. The deer bounded out of sight.

When I turned again the water was roaring into the boat. I was being pressed hard into the bank.

"Loosen the rope! Tell him, George!" I yelled.

George shouted in Spanish and Pepe promptly dropped the rope in the water. That was the worst thing he could have done.

"Grab the bow! Don't let it swing out!" I ordered.

The bow swung out into the current before George could reach it, and I was helpless. I struggled to get out of where I was wedged. But I could not budge. In a kind of despair that saw all of the outfit lost, I hung on to the boat and bawled for Pepe to get the rope. Pepe plunged into the swift current, caught the rope, and then went under. The boat swung around and, now half full of water, got away from me. I leaped out on the ledge and ran along with the boat. It gathered headway, careened round the curve, and shot down. Pepe was still under.

"He's drowned! he's drowned!" cried George.

I had a sickening sense of that when suddenly Pepe appeared like a brown porpoise. He was touching the bottom in places and holding back on the rope. Then the current rolled him over and over. Before I had an idea of how to avert the impending loss the boat drifted back of a rocky point and sank close to the shore in more than two feet of water. As I plunged in, my grip containing camera, films, and other perishable goods was the only thing not out of sight, and it was sinking. I rescued it about half soaked, and threw it upon the rocks. Pepe came up, still holding to the rope, and I towed him out of the current. Together we lifted the boat and hauled the bow up on the shore.

"Pretty lucky!" I exclaimed, with relief so deep I had to sit down and laugh. "Lift out the stuff, Pepe."

"Pretty tough luck!" growled George. He jerked open his grip and, throwing out articles of wet clothing—for which he had no concern—he gazed in dismay at his whole store of cigarettes ruined by the water.

"Young man, I'll have something to say to you presently," I said, severely.

Nothing had been carried from the boat. That part of our supplies which would be affected by water had been packed in tin cases and so suffered no damage. The ammunition was waterproof. But both my Parker hammerless and .351 automatic Winchester were full of water. I took them apart and laid the pieces in the sun. While I was occupied Pepe spread out the rest of the outfit, and then baled out the boat. The sun was so hot that the things dried quickly, and we lost scarcely an hour by the accident. Before we started I took good occasion to lecture Pepe and George, and when I got through they were both very sober and quiet.

I observed, however, that by the time we had run the next rapids they were enjoying themselves again. We had a long succession of rapids which we shot without anything approaching a mishap. When we drifted into the level stretch Pepe relieved me at the oars. We glided downstream under the drooping bamboos, under the silken streamers of silvery moss, under the dark cool bowers of matted vine and blossoming creepers. And as we passed this time the jungle silence awoke to the crack of George's guns and the discordant cry of river fowl. My guns were both at my hand, and the rifle was loaded, but I did not use either. I contented myself with snapping a picture here and there and watching the bamboo thickets and the mouths of the little dry ravines.

That ride was again so interesting, so full of sound and action and color, that it seemed a very short one. The murmur of water on the rocks told me that it was time to change seats with Pepe. We drifted down two short rapids and then came to the gravelly channels between the islands we had noted on the way up. The water was shallow down these rippling channels, and fearing we might strike a rock I tumbled out over the bow and, wading slowly, let the boat down till we came to still water again. I was about to get in when I espied what I thought was an alligator lying along a log near the river. I pointed it out to Pepe.

"Iguana!" he exclaimed, in delight, and reached for his machete.

The reptile was several feet long, blue black on top, and, with the exception of a blunt rounded head, had semblance to an alligator.

"Don't shoot. I'll get him," whispered Pepe, slipping out of the boat. He began to wade ashore, when the iguana raised its head. That was too much for George, who promptly shot at it. The reptile flopped off the log and started up the bank with Pepe in hot pursuit, brandishing his machete. Remarkably awkward as that iguana was, he could surely cover ground with his stumpy legs. Pepe got

A GIANT MANGROVE TREE

EVERGLADE SEMINOLE INDIAN IN NATIVE CANOE

Z. G. AND R. C. ON THE WAY TO THE TARPON GROUNDS

MILES UP THE WINDING CHANNELS

close enough once and he swung his weapon. The blow cut off a piece of the long tail, but the only effect it produced was to make the beast run faster. They appeared in the brush, and presently Pepe reappeared, having given up the chase. The iguana could be heard crashing through the dry thickets. Pepe returned to the boat, covered with ticks, and much concerned at the failure to capture the big lizard, which he said made fine eating.

Shortly after that we passed the scene of our first camp and then drifted under the railroad bridge. George and Pepe looked as if they were occupied with the same thought I had—that once beyond the railroad bridge we would plunge into the jungle wilderness and there could be no turning back. As we rounded a bend I was both sorry and glad to see the bridge vanish.

The Santa Rosa opened out wide and ran swiftly over smooth stone. Deep cracks, a foot or so wide, crossed the river diagonally. Fish darted in and out of these. We had about half a mile of this, when, after turning a hilly bend, we entered a long rapid. The water was still swift and smooth and shallow. There was scarcely a wave or ripple. At times the boat stuck fast on the flat rock and we had to get out and to shove off. As far ahead as I could see extended this wide slant of water. On the left rose a thick line of huge cypresses all festooned with gray moss that drooped to the river; on the right a bare bluff of crumbling rock reared itself. It looked like blue clay baked and cracked by the sun. A few palms fringed the top.

After getting out of the boat a dozen times or more it occurred to me that I might save energy. So I sat on the bow with my feet in the water. The little channels ran every way, and it was necessary to turn the boat often,

which I did with a kick of my foot.   Then we drifted along,
whirling round and round.   Occasionally Pepe would drop
his brown foot in and kick his end of the craft off a shallow
ledge.   It dawned upon me that here was a new and unique
way to travel downstream.   It was different from anything
I had ever tried before.

The water was swift and seldom deeper than a foot,
except in the cracks that ribbed the level river bed.   Fish
were so numerous that I kicked at many as they passed or
darted under the boat.   There were thousands of small
ones and many large.   Occasionally a big fellow would
make the water roar as he lunged into a crack.   There was
a fish that resembled a mullet, and some kind of a bass with
a blue tail.   This fish was so swift and I saw so many that
would weigh five pounds or more, that I pointed up my
small rod and, putting on a spinner, began to cast it about.
I felt two light fish hit it and then a heavy shock that mo-
mentarily checked the drifting boat.   The water split in a
streaky splash, and I was just about to jump off to follow
the fish when it broke the leader.   Then I tried a fly without
getting a strike.   By way of variety George shot at several
of the blue-tailed bass—if such they were—and he made
them jump out of the water like a real northern bronze-
back.

This long shut-in stretch appeared to be endless.   But for
the swift movement of the boat, which created a little
breeze, the heat would have been intolerable.   I was glad
to be wet.   The cool water sent thrills over me.   Little
clouds of steam rose from all of us.   I began to think I
had been wise in boiling the water we drank and in dosing
out quinine and anti-malaria pills from the start.   We all
suffered from a parching thirst.   Pepe scooped water up in

his hand; George would have followed suit had I not stopped him. Finally we squeezed the juice of a lime into a cup of water and drank that.

We drifted five miles under the glaring sun, and still the bare blue bluff persisted, and the line of gray-veiled cypresses, and the strange formation of stream bed. During all that distance I sat on the bow seat, occasionally kicking the boat off a ledge and whirling it around. The ride was novel and strange, but at last the sameness of it palled upon me. I wondered when we would come to the end of this hot stretch and once more enter the cool, shady jungle.

"Buck! buck!" whispered Pepe, suddenly, pointing down along the shore.

I saw a fine big deer leap back from the water and start to climb the side of a gully that indented the bluff. Snatching up the .351, I shoved in the safety catch. The distance was far—perhaps two hundred and fifty yards—but I let drive without elevating the sights. A cloud of dust puffed up under the nose of the climbing buck. He leaped up the steep winding trail, his white flag standing, his reddish coat glistening. That shot gave me the range, and I pulled the automatic again—again—again. Each bullet sent up a white puff, each nearer the deer. I held a little firmer and finer at the space ahead of him and pressed the trigger twice. The buck went down, slipped off the trail and, raising a cloud of dust, rolled over and over, and then, falling sheer into space, struck the rock with a sodden crash.

We drifted down a little and, wading, pulled the boat to shore. Pepe pronounced the buck to be very large, but it appeared small to me. The bullet that had stopped it had gone through the neck near the shoulder. If there was an unbroken bone left in that deer I would greatly miss my guess. We cut out the haunch the least crushed by the fall, and resumed our drifting down the river. How remarkable it was for me to see buzzards circling down before we had gone half a mile! These birds of prey did not fly from the country on either side of the river. They sailed, dropped down from the blue sky where they had been invisible. I watched them soaring and circling till a curve in the river hid them from view.

And with this bend came a welcome change. The bluff played out in a rocky bench beyond which the green jungle was relief to aching eyes. As we made this point the evening breeze started to blow. We beached the boat here and unloaded to make camp.

III

SHOOTING RAPIDS

WE were fortunate in finding a grassy plot where ticks and other creeping things appeared few. This evening it was a little annoying to me to realize how I had begun to feel uncomfortably sensitive about these ticks. We pitched camp in short order, but were interrupted immediately.

Pepe went up the bank for firewood. We heard him slashing away with his machete. Then this sound ceased; there followed a silence, at length broken by a yell. George and I both caught up guns and bounded into the thicket. I led the way, calling out to Pepe, and, crashing through a thorny brake, came suddenly upon him. At the same instant I caught a glimpse of gray, black-striped forms

R. C. HOOKS A BIG ONE. FIRST LEAP—CLOSE

SECOND LEAP

slipping away into the jungle. Pepe shouted out something.

"Tiger-cats!" exclaimed George.

"Quiet now," I whispered.

With that I stole forward cautiously, Pepe and George coming noiselessly at my heels. The thicket was lined with well-beaten trails, and by following these and stooping low it was possible to go ahead without rustling the brush. I could not see very far, owing to the gathering twilight. When we stopped to listen we heard a cracking of dead brush some distance off. Concluding the tiger-cats had gotten safely out of sight, I turned to go back to camp. We had not proceeded far when soft pattering footsteps halted me. Peering down one of the paths, I saw a cat. I was amazed at its boldness. Surely it heard us, and instead of bounding into the thicket crouched in the path not twenty-five feet from me. I took a quick shot at the gray huddled form. It jerked spasmodically, stretched, and lay still. I held the boys back a moment, then we advanced to find the cat dead. It was bigger than any wild cat I had ever seen. The color was a grayish yellow, almost white, lined and spotted with black. It was heavy enough to make a good load for Pepe.

"Pepe says there are two or three kinds of cats besides the big tiger," remarked George, "and we may run into a lot of them. We ought to get some dandy skins."

It was almost dark when we got back to camp. Part of our supper was burnt, but that did not interfere with our enjoyment of it. We were very hungry and tired and pleased with the events of the day. As we sat around the camp fire there was a constant whirring of water fowl over our heads, and an incessant hum of insects from the jungle.

Pepe made a good job of skinning the tiger-cat, and I stretched the skin on a framework of sticks and salted it. I anticipated difficulty in preserving skins in that hot climate. Then we went to bed, very grateful for the cool breeze and for the absence of mosquitoes.

Upon awakening I found the sun an hour high; I was stiff and sore and thirsty. Pepe and Allen slept so soundly it seemed selfish to awaken them. About camp there was a melodious concourse of birds, but the parrots did not visit us that morning. While I was washing in the river a troop of deer came down to a bar upon the opposite side. I ran for my rifle and by mistake took up George's .32. I had a splendid shot at less than one hundred yards, but the ball dropped fifteen feet in front of the leading buck. The deer ran into the deep bushy willows. Pepe jumped up and George rolled out of his blanket with one eye still glued shut. Telling them to cook breakfast, I took my gun and started off to climb the high river bluff.

It was my idea to look out over the surrounding country and get the lay of the land. The matter of climbing the bluff would have been easy but for the fact that I wished to avoid contact with the grass, brush, trees, even dead branches, as all were covered with ticks. The upper half of the bluff was bare, and when I reached that part I soon surmounted it.

I faced south with something of eagerness. Fortunately the mist had dissolved under the warm rays of the sun, affording an unobstructed view. That scene was wild and haunting, yet different from what fancy had pictured. The great expanse of jungle was gray, the green line of cypress, palm and bamboo following the southward course of the river. The mountain range some ten miles distant sloped to the south and faded away in the haze. The river disappeared in rich dark verdure, and but for it I would have been lost in a dense gray-green overgrowth of tropical wilderness. Once or twice I thought I caught a faint roar of waterfall on the morning breeze, yet I could not be sure, and I returned toward camp with a sober appreciation of the difficulty of my enterprise and a more thrilling sense of its hazard and charm.

Soon we were under way again, Pepe strong and willing at the oars, George keen-eyed for something to shoot at. This time I had my rifle and shotgun close at hand, ready for use. Half a mile below, the river running still and deep, we entered a shaded waterway so narrow that in places the branches of wide-spreading and leaning cypresses met and intertwined their moss-fringed foliage. This lane was a paradise for birds that ranged from huge speckled cranes, six feet high, to little yellow birds almost too small to see. George kept popping away with his .22 and soon had several chicalocki and two ducks. Black squirrels were numerous and very tame. In fact, all the creatures along this shaded stream were so fearless that it was easy to see they had never been shot at. I woke sleepy cranes with my fishing rod and once pushed a blue heron off a log. We heard animals of some species running back from the bank, but could not see them.

All at once a soft breeze coming upstream bore a deep roar of tumbling waters. For an instant I had a sensation of utter dread. For that roar was a familiar one to me and I knew what it meant. A canoeist learns, long before he comes to rapids, to judge what they are from the sound. The heavy, sullen roar, almost a rumble, took my attention from the beautiful birds, the moss-shaded bowers, and the overhanging jungle.

"That water sounds different," remarked George.

"Yes, I guess it does," I replied, grimly, and began to pack my guns away in their cases.

Pepe rowed on and George popped away with his .22, both unconscious of the menace in that dull, continuous sound. But I knew we were soon to drop into the real wilderness and that there could be no turning back. Keeping a sharp lookout ahead, I revolved in my mind the necessity for caution and skillful handling of the boat. But I realized, too, the incongruous fact that too much care, an overzealousness on the side of precaution, was even less of an asset for such a trip than sheer recklessness. Good judgment in looking over the rapids, a quick seizing of the best way to get through, then a spirit the opposite of timidity—that is the ideal to be striven for.

Presently there was a break in the level surface of the river. The banks were low and shelved out in rocky points. This relieved me, for I saw that we could land just above the falls. What I feared most was a narrow gorge impossible to portage round or go through. As we approached the break the roar seemed to divide itself, hollow and shallow near at hand, rushing and heavy farther on.

Pepe rowed close to the bank and landed on the first strip of rock. We got out and, walking along this ledge, soon reached the fall. It was a straight drop of some ten or twelve feet. The water was shallow all the way across. This passage seemed to present no difficulty beyond carrying around the supplies and outfit. But there was white water below the fall as far as I could see. From here came the roar that had perturbed me.

Portaging the outfit around that fall turned out to be a job I hoped we would not have to repeat. The portage was not long nor very rugged, but the cracked rock made going very disagreeable. The boys stumbled often; Pepe fell and broke open a box, and I had a hard knock. There was a wide shelving apron below the fall, over which the water ran a foot or so in depth. I stationed George and Pepe here, then went up to get the boat. I waded out with it, ran the stern over the drop, bore down hard on the bow, and shoved off. The boat went down with a flop and did not ship a cupful of water. Pepe caught it and waded to the lower ledge, where we had carried our things. Here we packed carefully.

I went downstream a little way to take a look at the rapids. They were just bad enough to make it hard work to avoid accidents. If the country had been such that damage to boat or supplies could have been replaced I would have gone at those rapids with delight. As it was I could not keep from worrying. I walked up and down, looked over the rapids more than was wise, and still hesitated about going into them. But it had to be done, so I finally took the oars with gripping fingers and backed the boat downstream.

To my right in the middle of the narrow river was a racy current that I kept out of as long as possible. But presently I was drawn into it and the boat shot forward, headed into the first incline, and went sliding smoothly down toward the white waves of the rapids. This was a trying moment for me. When we thumped into the back-lash of the first big wave the water thrashed round and over the boys. Then we were in the thick of roar and rush. I knew I was not handling the boat well. We grazed rocks that should have been easy to avoid, and bumped on hidden ones, and got half broadside of the current. Pepe, by quick action with an oar, pushed the stern aside from collision with more than one rock. Several times I missed a stroke when a powerful one was needed. We passed between stones so close together that I had to ship the oars. It was all rapid water, this stretch, but the bad places with sunken rocks, falls and big waves were strung out at such distances apart that I always got the boat going right before we went into them.

I saw hardly anything of the banks of the river. They blurred in my sight, but sometimes they were near, sometimes far. We turned corners where rocky ledges pointed out, constricting the stream and making a curve. What lay round the curve was always a question and a cause for supreme suspense. More than once we raced down a chute and straight into a rocky wall, against which Pepe would strike his oar hard.

Several times Pepe narrowly escaped being knocked overboard. I tried to get him not to stand up. Finally at the foot of a long rapid I was drifting with the current when Pepe stood up and yelled. There was a stone directly in our way and I dropped the oars into the water with a quick jerk. Pepe shot out of the stern as if he had been flung from a catapult. He swam with the current while I drifted and backed the boat toward him, but he reached smooth water and the shore before I could pick him up.

We had a good laugh all around. There were three inches of water in the boat, but the canvas had protected our grips and supplies. George and I were almost as wet as Pepe. With that long rapid behind me I felt different. It was what I had needed. My nervousness disappeared and I had no dread of the next drop or anything that lay before us. While Pepe and George baled out the boat I rested and meditated on the change in my feelings. I had made mistakes in that rapid just passed. Luck had favored me. I went over the mistakes and saw where I had been wrong and how I could have avoided them. This was a dare-devil trip, and the dare-devil in me had not been liberated. It took just the nervous dread, hard work, blunders and accidents, danger and luck to unleash the spirit which alone could make such a trip a success. Pepe and George by this time had a blind faith in me. They could scarcely appreciate the real hazard of our undertaking and I had no desire to impart it to them.

Then we were on our way again, and it was no surprise to hear a dull roar round the next bend. But this time, though the hair rose stiff under my hat, I did not feel the chill, the uncertainty, the lack of confidence that had before weakened me.

A turn in the winding lane of cypresses revealed walls of gray rock between which the river disappeared. At the head of the ravine we found a long shallow incline. We tumbled overboard and with Pepe and George at the stern and me at the bow we waded down. The water tore round our legs and rose higher and higher. Soon the boys had to jump aboard, but I held to the bow an instant longer, then leaped on and made for the oars. I got them, and just in time for a strong pull on the left which righted the boat when we hit the waves. At the bottom of these swift inclines was always a chaos of leaping green and white curlers. The blunt stern of the boat made a great splash and the spray flew over us. We came out of the roar and hiss and smoke to drift into a mill-race current. I had never seen such long inclines of swift water as we were meeting. This one terminated in a sullen plunge between two huge rocks. It was no place to take a boat, but one glance assured me there was no other way. George yelled and Pepe's eyes started from his head when I backed down that chute. Down! with the speed of the wind; then we were raised aloft, light as a feather, to crash into the back-lashers. The din deafened me, the spray blinded me —and we were out again among the little choppy waves, soon to glide into another long smooth runway.

So we passed rapid after rapid, all connected by slanting channels of swift water. Such formation of stream-bed was new and strange to me. But I had scarcely time to enjoy the ride between the waterfalls, and, when we were in the midst of the green billowy ways with here and there ugly rocks splitting the current, I had work on my hands.

It dawned on me, during a breathing spell, that I had lost count of the rapids. The last I remembered was number eleven, then far, far behind. By and by we came to a bold rocky bluff around which the river split. Which branch to take was a matter of conjecture. Evidently this bluff was an island. It had a yellow front and long bare ledges leading into the river. Leaving the boat, we climbed the bluff to find it covered with palm trees. Up there it was so hot and dry that it did not seem to be jungle at all. Even the palm leaves were yellow and parched. I could not bear the heat. We took one look at the surrounding country, so wild and dry and still, and then clambered down the loose, dusty shelves.

Then we surveyed the right branch of the river and followed it a little way. The stream here foamed and swirled among jagged rocks. At the foot of this rapid stretched

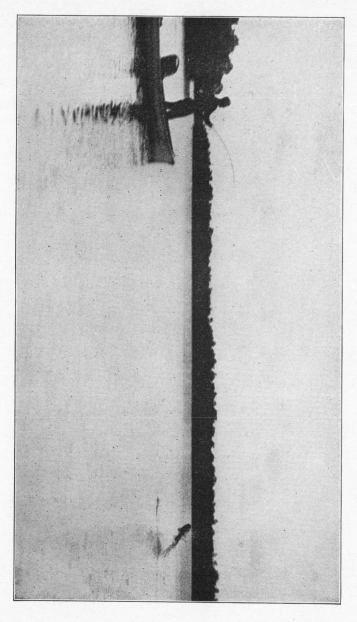

THIRD LEAP

FIFTEENTH LEAP OVER ONE HUNDRED YARDS FROM BOAT

the first dead water we had encountered for miles. A flock of wild geese rose from under our feet and flew downstream.

We returned to look at the left branch. It was open and one continuous succession of low steps. That would have decided me, even if the greater volume of water had not gone down on this side. As far as we could see was a wide stream, running over little ledges. It promised the easiest and swiftest navigation we had come upon, and so indeed it proved. The water flowed rapidly and always dropped over some ledge in a rounded fall that was safe for us to shoot. It was great fun going over these places. We hung our feet over the gunwales most of the time, sliding them along the slippery ledge or giving a kick to help the momentum. When we came to a fall I would drop off at the bow, hold the boat back and swing it straight, then jump in, and over we would go—souse!

There were so many of these ledges and they were so close together that repetition engendered carelessness, and once we almost had a wreck. But I saved the boat on the verge of a fall more than four feet high. I held on while the swift water surged up to my knees, and I yelled for the boys to jump off. As the stern where they sat was already over the fall it was somewhat difficult to make them vacate quickly enough.

"Tumble out! Quick, idiots!" I bawled.

Over they went, up to their necks in the boiling foam, and not a second too soon, for I could hold the boat no longer. It went over smoothly, just dipping the stern under water. If the boys had remained aboard the boat would have swamped. As it was, Pepe managed to catch the rope which I had thrown out, and he drifted down to the next ledge. We found this nearly as high as the last one. So I sent the boys below to catch the boat. This plan worked well. The shelves slanted slightly with the shallow part of the water just at the break of the ledge. We passed half a dozen of these, making good time, and before we knew it we were again in a deep, smooth jungle lane with bamboo and streamers of moss waving over us.

The shade was cool, and I settled down in the stern seat, grateful for the rest. To my surprise, I did not see a bird. The jungle was asleep. Once or twice I fancied I heard the gurgle and tinkle of water running over rocks. We glided along silently, Pepe rowing leisurely as if weary, George asleep, and I dreamily watching the beautiful green banks. They were high, a mass of big-leafed vines, flowering and fragrant, above which towered the jungle giants. This was by far the most beautiful strip of river we had navigated. I was reveling in the cool recesses under the leaning cypresses, in the soft swish of bearded moss and the rustle of palms, in the dreamy hum of that resting jungle, when my pleasure was brought to an abrupt end.

"Santa Maria!" yelled Pepe. In moments of excitement he often called aloud the names of saints or the Virgin.

I came out of my trance. The boat was stuck in a mud bank. That branch of the river ended right there. We had come all these miles only to run into a blind pocket. One glance at the high yellow bank, here crumbling and bare, told me there was no outlet. George rubbed his eyes and, searching for a cigarette, muttered: "I said it was coming to us. We've got to go back."

IV

CYPRESS ISLAND

PEPE shoved off the oozy mud, and reluctantly, as if he, too, appreciated the nature of upstream travel, turned the boat and began to row back. As soon as I recovered from my momentary chagrin I thought of the volume of water that rushed down on this side of the island and wondered where it went. That it sank into the earth or had an underground passageway was so improbable that it was not worth considering. I decided there was an outlet which we had missed.

I ordered Pepe to row close to the bank on what I thought was the island side; and as we glided along under the drooping bamboos and the silky curtains of moss George kept calling out, "Low bridge!" There were places where we had to lie flat, and others where Pepe was called upon to use his machete. We disturbed the siesta of many aquatic birds. Most of them flew swiftly up or down the stream. But there were many of the gray breasted, blue-backed bitterns that did not take to flight. These croaked dismally and looked down upon us with their strange protruding eyes.

"Boys, I hear running water," I said, suddenly, and signaled Pepe to stop rowing. "Aha! There's a current too. See! it's making right under this bank."

Before us was a high wall of broad-leaved vines, so thick that nothing could be seen through them. Apparently this luxuriant canopy concealed the bank. Pepe poked into it with an oar, and encountered nothing solid.

"Pepe, use your machete and cut a way through. I want to see where this water runs."

It was then that I came to a full appreciation of the wonderful use of a machete. Pepe flashed the long black blade up and down and around, and presently the boat was its own length in a green tunnel. We got through this mass of foliage and, much to our surprise, found no high bank at all, but low flat ground, densely wooded, through which ran a narrow deep outlet of the stream. The boat glided into it without any guidance.

"Well!"

George and Pepe supplemented my exclamation with fervid remarks. Then we all fell silent. The deep penetrating stillness of that jungle was not provocative of speech. The shade was so black that when a ray of sunlight did manage to pierce the dense canopy overhead it resembled a brilliant golden spear. A few lofty palms and a few clumps of bamboo rather emphasized the lack of these particular species in this forest. Nor was there any of the familiar streaming moss hanging from the trees. This glen was green, cool, dark. It did not smell exactly swampy, but rank, like a place where many water plants were growing.

The outlet was so narrow that we were not able to use the oars. Still, as the current was swift, we went along rapidly. I saw a light ahead and heard the babble of water. The current quickened. We drifted suddenly upon the edge of an oval glade where the hot sun beat down. A series of abrupt mossy benches, over which the stream slid almost noiselessly, blocked further progress.

The first thing about this glade that I noted particularly, after the difficulty presented by the steep steps, was the

TIRED TARPON ROLLING

TARPON SWERVING UNDER BOAT

number of snakes sunning themselves along the line of our future progress.

"Boys, it'll be fun wading down there, won't it?" I said.

Pepe grumbled his displeasure. He was afraïd of snakes, and to judge from the way George began to pop around with his .22 he had no love for them. As for myself, I had doubts about this particular kind of snake. He was short, thick, rather dull brown, and the way he disappeared in the stream proved he was a watersnake. If he belonged to the dreaded moccasin family I did not recognize the kinship. Anyway, snakes were the least of my troubles.

I walked down through the glade into the forest again, and was overjoyed to hear once more the heavy roar of rapids. I went through to see the gleam of water through the trees.

"All right, boys," I sang out. "There's the river."

We were so immensely relieved that packing the outfit round the waterfalls of the glen was work that we set about with alacrity. Pepe, being barefoot, wasted considerable time looking for snakes down the fern-lined trail we broke. We made our last trip with supplies, and I was about to start back to solve the problem of getting the boat down when Pepe let out a yell that resounded through the sleeping jungle. Parrots screeched and there was a cackling of other birds.

I followed the direction of Pepe's staring eyes and trembling finger. Hanging from a limb of a tree just across the glade was a huge black snake. It was as thick as my leg. I was too frightened to estimate its length. But the branch upon which it poised so gracefully was at least ten feet from the ground.

"Holy smoke!" cried George, diving into the pack for

his gun. Pepe began to jabber. I could not understand what he said, but did not need his excitement to tell me that this was a dangerous snake. I had been warned to look out for this fellow.

"Here, George, not your rifle," I said, "you can't hit him with that. Get your shotgun."

But the sixteen-gauge was clogged with a shell which would not eject. My guns were in their cases. George handed me his .32.

Twice I shot at the head of the snake. It was a slow-swaying mark, hard to hit. How wonderfully the reptile poised on that limb! He was not coiled round it, but lay over it with about four feet of his length waving, swaying to and fro, and he was watching us with most sinister intent.

It was only natural, however rash, for me to send a bullet through the thick part of his body. Swift as a streak of lightning he darted from the limb.

"Look out, fellows!" I yelled. George ran after Pepe, who had already retreated, and I, catching up the machete, got out of that vicinity with undignified haste. How far we would have run had the snake pursued us was something worth conjecture. But he probably was as badly scared as we were. Cautiously we returned to the glade and found blood stains on the ground under the tree. The snake had disappeared without leaving a trail.

"If I'd had my shotgun ready," I exclaimed in disgust, and I made a note that as I had come into the jungle to shoot I would do well in the future to be prepared.

"Boys, you drive away those little snakes while I figure on a way to get the boat down," I said.

I went back to the top of the glade, where we had left

the boat, but I did not do much figuring till George and Pepe had accomplished the task imposed upon them. Armed with long poles they whacked and threshed and yelled; and everywhere along the wet benches slipped and splashed the brown snakes. Then the boys helped me lower the boat over the first fall. This done, I studied the situation before me.

There was a succession of benches through which the stream zigzagged and tumbled. These benches were rock ledges over which moss had grown fully a foot thick, and they were so oozy and slippery that it was no easy task to walk upon them. Then they were steep, so steep that it was remarkable how the water ran over them so smoothly, with very little noise or break. It was altogether a new kind of waterfall to me. But if the snakes had not been hidden there navigation would have presented an easier problem.

"Come on, boys, alongside now, and hold back," I ordered, gripping the bow.

Exactly what transpired the next few seconds was not clear in my mind. There was a rush, and we were being dragged by the boat. The glade seemed to whiz past me. There were some sodden thumps, a great splashing, a check —and, lo! we were over several benches. It was the quickest and easiest descent I had ever made down a steep waterfall.

"Fine!" ejaculated George, wiping the ooze from his face.

"Yes, it was fine," I replied. "But unless this boat has wings something 'll happen soon."

Below us was a long, swift curve of water, very narrow and steep, with a moss-covered rock dividing the lower end. It bothered me. If we had a repetition of the first descent

we might find the boat smashed on that rock. Sending
Pepe below to take his station there and so render less
likely the danger of collision, I gave George orders to help
me.

Gently, gingerly we started the boat off the bench where
it had lodged. George was at the stern, I at the bow, and
we were both on the right of the stream. The boat dipped,
then—wheeze! it dived over the bench. George went
sprawling clear off the bank into the stream. I had the
bow rope coiled round my hands. I howled for help and
held on for dear life. If I retarded the progress of the boat
it was not enough to allow George to catch up with us. He
made a valiant effort, but a few leaps and a short dash
after us ended in disaster for him. His feet flew up higher
than his head; he actually turned over in the air and fell
with a great sop. Despite my fear of snakes, and the
greater fear for the boat, I let out a peal of laughter. Then
my mouth filled with nasty water that nearly strangled me.
I was blinded, too. My arms seemed to be wrenched out
of their sockets and I felt myself bumping over moss-
covered rocks as soft as cushions. It was impossible to
hold the rope any longer. I lodged against a stone and
the water forced me upon it, where, blinking and coughing,
I stuck fast. I saw the boat headed like an arrow for the
stone where Pepe stood. He had his hands outstretched to
stop it. I feared for his life and would have yelled if there
had been time. At the last second Pepe turned tail to get
out of the way, but he slipped and fell. The boat shot
toward him, and the blunt stern, rising on the swell of
water, struck him with a dull thud. Pepe sailed into the
air, over the rock, and cleaved the stream in a beautiful
dive. The boat slipped over the stone as easily as if it

had been a wave, and, gliding into the still water below, lodged on the bank.

Then I knew the boat was not hurt, nor the boys, nor I. I knew also why the boat had developed such bewildering speed. The current was much swifter than it appeared and the moss on the stones was more slippery than an eel. When I got to the bank there were Pepe and George, the former like a drowned rat, and George not recognizable in his coating of slime. I stretched myself on the ground and gave up to mirth.

It spoke well for their sense of humor that the boys were able to join me in a good laugh. Then, seeing that the snakes had reappeared, we lost no time in repacking the boat and proceeding upon our way. Meeting with no further obstacle, we drifted out of the shady jungle once more into the sunlit river. Just above the mouth of the little outlet was a roaring rapids that made me catch my breath.

"*Mucha malo*," remarked Pepe, who meant that was very bad.

We had half a mile of swift current, and in that distance our clothes dried out in the heat of the sun. The water fairly smoked, it was so hot. Once more we entered a placid aisle over which the magnificent gray-wreathed cypresses bowed, and the west wind waved long ribbons of moss, and wild fowl winged reluctant flight before us.

Beyond the first bend in the river we came upon an island with a narrow shaded channel on one side, a wide shoal on the other. A group of cypresses stood at the upstream end. The instant I saw the island I knew that it was the place I had long been seeking to make permanent camp for a few days. We landed to find an ideal camping site. The ground under the cypresses was flat, dry and covered with a

short turf. Not a ray of sunlight penetrated the foliage.
A huge pile of driftwood had lodged against one of the
trees, and this made easy the question of firewood. The
island was about two hundred yards long and the lower
end was hidden from us by a scant growth of willows.
Bursting through this we found a shallow weedy flat where
great numbers of ducks were sporting and feeding. The
stones of the rocky shore were covered with sleeping water
fowl. Our advent created a commotion; there was a great
clapping of wings and squawking. But at least half the
number of ducks and other water fowl did not fly. And
the best feature of this beautiful island was that we did not
see a snake or a tick.

"Boys, this is the place," I said. "We'll hang up here
awhile."

So we unloaded the boat, taking everything out, and
proceeded to make a camp that, compared with our former
efforts, was simply a delight. When we had accomplished
our labors we were unanimous in our expressions of satisfaction. Then Pepe set about leisurely peeling potatoes;
George took his gun and slipped off toward the lower end
of the island, and I made a comfortable lounging bed
under a cypress.

Bing! bang! went George's gun. A loud whirring of
wings followed, and the air was thick with ducks. A flock
of teal skimmed the water and disappeared upstream.
The shots awakened the parrots in the trees, and for a time
there was clamor. I saw George wade out into the shoal
and pick up three ducks, so evidently he had made a pot-
shot. Then he crossed to the opposite bank and, climbing
a bare place, stood looking before him. I called to him

not to go far, and presently he passed into the bushes out of sight.

I lay back upon my blanket with a blissful sense of rest and contentment. Many a time I had lain so, looking up through the broad leaves of a sycamore, or the lacy foliage of a birch, or the delicate criss-cross of millions of pine needles. This overhead canopy, however, was different. Only here and there could I catch little shivers of blue sky. The graceful streamers of exquisite moss hung like tassels of silver. In the dead stillness of noonday they seemed to float, curved in the shape in which the last soft breeze had left them. High upon a branch a red-headed parrot was hanging back downward, after the fashion of a monkey. Then there were two parrots asleep in a fork of a branch. It was the middle of the day and all things seemed tired and sleepy.

The deep channel murmured drowsily, and the wide expanse of river on the other side lapped lazily at the shore. The only other sound was the mourning of turtledoves, one near and another far away. Again the full richness, the mellow sweetness of this bird song struck me forcibly. I remembered that all the way down the river I had heard that mournful note. It was beautiful but melancholy. Somehow it made me think that it had broken the dreamy stillness of the jungle noonday long, long before the birth of man. It was sweet, but sad and old. I did not like to hear it.

I yielded to the soothing influence of the hour and fell asleep. When I awoke there was George standing partially undressed, and very soberly popping ticks. He had enlisted the services of Pepe, and to judge from the remarks of both they needed still more assistance.

"Say, Garrapato George, many ticks over there?"

"Ticks!" shouted George, wildly waving his cigarette. "Millions of 'em! And there's—— Ouch! Kill that one, Pepe. Wow! He's as big as a penny. . . . There's game over there. There's lots of trails. I saw cat tracks and I scared up wild turkeys——"

"Turkeys!" I exclaimed, eagerly.

"You bet. I saw a dozen. Gee! they can run! I didn't flush them. Then I saw a flock of those black-and-white ducks, like the big fellow I shot. They were feeding. I believe they're Muscovy ducks."

"I'm sure I don't know, but we can call them that."

"Well, I'd got a shot, too, but I saw some gray things sneaking in the bushes. I thought they were pigs, so I got out of there quick."

"You mean *javelin?*"

"Yep, I mean wild pigs. Oh, we've struck the place for game! I'll bet it's coming to us."

One of the nicest things about George was his fatalistic anticipation of forthcoming events. He was always expecting something to happen, and most of the time he looked forward with great eagerness.

"We'll hunt, George, ticks or no ticks," I said, and went back to my lounging.

When I came out of that lazy spell George was assiduously fishing, and he remarked on the number of fish breaking water all about us. Where a little while before the river had been smooth, it was now ruffled by ravalo and other fish I did not know. But we could not get them to bite. We tried artificial flies, spoons, and minnows, then some of the mullet we had brought along for tarpon fishing farther down, and all kinds of meat baits. With little and big fish capering around under our very noses it was exasperating not to be able to hook one. I shot a small one, not unlike a pickerel in shape, especially in the long bill mouth, and we baited with that. Still we were not rewarded by a strike. This put me on my mettle, so I went to the lower end of the island and, rigging up a minnow tackle, tried to catch some minnows. There were plenty of them, but they would not bite. Finally I began to wade in the shallow water and turn over the stones. I found snails almost as large as mussels. With these I went back to George and told him to try one.

George complied. No sooner had the bait sunk than he got a strong pull. He jerked up, hooking a fish that made the rod look like a buggy-whip. I tried to get it away from him. But he held on and hauled with all his might. A long finely built fish, green as emerald, split the water with a thump, churned it into foam, then, sweeping away in a strong dash, broke my rod squarely off in the middle. It was a favorite rod that had served me for years, and I eyed the wreck of it with sorrow, and George with no little disapproval.

"George, you're a grand fisherman, grand—I don't think," I remarked.

"Those split bamboo rods are no good; they won't hold anything," was George's protest.

By four o'clock, when we sat down to our supper, I was so thirsty that my mouth puckered as dry as if I had been eating green persimmons. This matter of thirst had begun to be serious for me. Twice a day I had boiled a small pot of water, into which I mixed cocoa, sugar, and condensed milk, and that was all I drank. In spite of my repeated warnings Pepe and George continued to drink the water unboiled. We opened cans of vegetables and fruit on this occasion, and fared sumptuously. As usual, the meal was interrupted. A string of Muscovy ducks sailed up the river. George had a good shot at the tail end of the flock and missed. Then a line of cranes and herons passed along and over our island. When a small bunch of teal flew by, to be followed by several canvas-backs, I got out my hammerless. It was a fine gun, built for trap shooting and much too valuable for such a trip. My reason for bringing it was because it was a hard shooting gun. My former hunting for wild fowl in Mexico had been a failure, owing to a light field gun. On this occasion I had a variety of shells and chose first to try those loaded with No. $7\frac{1}{2}$ chilled shot and twenty-six grains of powder—a trap load.

While Pepe leisurely finished the supper, George and I sat upon the bank watching for ducks. Just before the sun went down a hard wind blew for a quarter of an hour, making difficult shooting, but after it died away we had capital sport. Every few moments ducks would whirl by. George's gun missed fire several times and he missed most of the ducks, and those he hit dropped a few feathers and sailed on.

To my surprise, I found the trap load exceedingly deadly, and I could reach ducks sometimes at a distance rudely calculated to be eighty yards. The little brown ducks and teal I stopped as if they had flown against a stone wall. I dropped a couple of the strong-winged canvas-backs in the dead plunge that a sportsman likes. A crippled duck is enough to make a man quit shooting. With six ducks killed, I decided to lay aside my gun for that time, when Pepe pointed down the river.

"*Pato real*," he whispered.

I looked eagerly and saw three of the big black ducks flying as high as the treetops and coming fast. Snapping a couple of shells in the gun, I stood ready. At the end of the island two of the birds wheeled to the left, but the big leader came on like a thunderbolt. It seemed to me he made a canvas-back look slow. I caught him over the sights of my gun, followed him up till he was even with me and beyond, then sweeping a little ahead of him I pulled both triggers. He swooped up and almost stopped in his flight while a cloud of black feathers puffed away on the wind. He sagged a little, recovered himself, and flew on as strong as ever. The No. 7½ chilled shot were not heavy enough to stop him.

"We'll need big shot for those ducks, and for the wild turkeys, too," said George.

"I've all sizes up to buckshot," I replied. "George, let's take a little stroll over where you saw the turkeys."

Pepe shook his head and said if we wanted to see game at this hour the thing to do was to sit still in camp and watch the game come down to the river to drink, and pointed downstream to a herd of small deer walking quietly out on a bar.

"After all the noise we made!" I exclaimed. "Well, this beats me! George, we'll stay right here and not shoot again to-night. I've an idea we'll see something worth while."

It was Pepe's idea, but I instantly saw its possibilities. There were no tributaries to the river or springs in that dry jungle, and as, manifestly, the whole country abounded in game, it must troop down to the river in the cool of the evening to allay the hot day's thirst. We were perfectly situated for watching the dark bank on the channel side of the island, as well as the open bars on the other. The huge cypresses cast shadows that even in daylight effectually concealed us. We put out the camp fire and, taking comfortable seats in the folds of the great gnarled roots, began to watch and listen.

The vanguard of thirsty deer had prepared me for something remarkable and I was in no wise disappointed. The trooping of deer down to the water's edge and the flight of wild fowl upstream increased in proportion to the gathering shadows of twilight. The deer must have scented us, for they raised their long ears and stood still as statues, gazing across toward the upper end of the island. But they exhibited no fear. It was only when they had drunk their fill and wheeled about to go up the narrow trails over the bank that they showed uneasiness and haste. This made me wonder if they were fearful of being ambushed by jaguars. Soon the dark line of deer along the shore shaded into the darkness of night. Then I heard soft splashes, and an occasional patter of hard hoofs. The whir of wings had ceased.

A low exclamation from Pepe brought my attention to interesting developments closer at hand.

"*Javelin!*" he whispered.

On the channel side of the island was impenetrable pitchy blackness. I tried to pierce it with straining eyes, but I could not make out even the shore line that I knew was only ten yards distant. Still I could hear, and that was thrilling enough. Everywhere on this side, along the edge of the water and up the steep bank, were faint tickings of twigs and soft rustlings of leaves. Then there was a continuous sound, so low as to be almost inaudible, that resembled nothing I could think of so much as a long line of softly dripping water. It swelled in volume to a tiny roll, and ended in a sharp clicking on rocks and a gentle splashing in the water. A drove of *javelin* had come down to drink. Occasionally the glint of green eyes made the darkness the more weird. Suddenly a long piercing wail, a keen cry almost human, quivered into the silence.

"Panther," I whispered instantly to the boys. It was a different cry from that of the lion of the Rockies, but there was a strange wild note that betrayed the species. A stillness fell, dead as that of a subterranean cavern. Strain my ears as I might, I could not detect the faintest sound. It was as if no *javelin* or any other animals had come down to drink. That listening, palpitating moment seemed endless. What mystery of wild life it meant, that silence following the cry of the panther. Then the jungle sounds recommenced—the swishing of water, the footsteps, the faint snapping of twigs. Some kind of cat let out an unearthly squall. Close upon this, the clattering of deer up the bank on the other side drew our sharp attention. The deer were running, and the striking of little hoofs ceased in short order. We listened intently. From far over the bank came a sound not unlike a cough, deep, hoarse, inexpressibly wild and menacing.

"*Tigre!*" cried Pepe, gripping me hard with both hands. I could feel him trembling, and had specific proof of how the native of the jungle-belt feared the jaguar.

Again the cough rasped out, nearer and louder this time. It was not a courage-provoking sound, and seemed on second thought more of a growl than a cough. I felt safe on the island; nevertheless I took up my rifle.

"That's a tiger," whispered George. "I heard one once from the porch of the Alamitas hacienda."

A third time the jaguar voiced his advent upon the night

scene; and this time if it was not a roar I have never heard one. But I was excited and a little frightened. I was reminded of my first experience in tarpon fishing, when I knew the tarpon was leaping and could see a silvery blur, but not the fish. I made up my mind to listen with clearer ears; however, the cough or roar was not repeated.

Moreover, a silence set in so unbroken that it seemed haunted by the echoes of those wild jungle cries. Perhaps I had the haunting echoes in my mind. I knew what had sent the deer away and stilled the splashings and creepings —it was the hoarse voice of the lord of the jungle.

Pepe, and George, too, were under the spell of the moment. We did not break that charm by talking. Giant fire-flies accentuated the ebony blackness, and the low hum of insects riveted the attention on the stillness. A great peace fell upon the jungle world. How wild it was! how wonderful! I understood then why, in the fever and turmoil of civilized pursuits, I was haunted by wild places. It was simply the longing to go back to some former stage of life's development. It was the intelligence of the developed man feeling the greater happiness of the unthinking savage who lived only in his world of sensorial perceptions.

The black mantle of night seemed to lift from under the trees, leaving a gloom that slowly paled. Through the dark branches, low down over the bank, appeared the white tropical moon. Shimmering gleams chased the shadows across the ripples, and slowly the river brightened to a silver sheen.

It only made the island more beautiful, lonely, and wild. The thought of leaving it gave me a pang. But I was chained to the haunts of men. The old wild order of life could come to me only in dreams and fleeting stolen moments such as this, when daring and endurance earned the semblance of a primitive day. It was only a hunting trip, this jaunt of mine, yet unquestionably, while it saddened me somehow, it strengthened my hold on better things.

And among them was the feeling of the wild places that I could never see, where the sun shone, the wind blew, the rain fell; where myriads of living things strove and died, and wild creatures evolved beings in the image of man; where year after year, century after century, night never fell but upon tragedy, and inevitable nature never changed her eternal plan.

V

MORE GAME

I awoke early in the morning, to a state of huge enjoyment. I was still lazily tired, but the dead drag and ache had gone from my bones. A cool breeze wafted the mist from the river, breaking it up into clouds, between which streamed rosy shafts of sunlight. Wood smoke from the fire Pepe was starting blew fragrantly over me. A hundred thousand birds seemed to be trying to burst their throats. The air was full of music. I lay still listening to this melodious herald of the day till it ceased.

Then a flock of parrots approached and circled over the island, screeching like a band of flying imps. Presently they alighted in the cypresses, bending the branches to a breaking point, and giving the trees a variegated spotted appearance of green and red. Pepe waved his hand toward another flock sweeping upon us.

"Parrakeets," he said.

These birds were a solid green, much smaller than the red-heads, with longer tails. They appeared wilder than the red-heads, and flew higher, circling the same way, and screeching, but they did not alight. Other flocks sailed toward us presently from all directions. The last one was a veritable cloud of parrots, a shining green and yellow mass several acres in extent. They flew still higher than the parrakeets.

"Yellow-heads!" shouted George in my ear. "They're the big fellows, the talkers. Gee! If there ain't a million of them!"

We ate breakfast in a din that made conversation useless. The red-heads swooped down upon our island, and the two unfriendly species flew over us, back and forth, manifestly trying to drive us away with their infernal racket. The mist had blown away, the sun was shining bright, and we were ready for our hunt when the myriads of parrots, in large and small flocks, departed to other jungle haunts.

We rowed across the wide shoal to the sand bars. There in the soft ooze, among the hundreds of deer tracks, I found a jaguar print larger than my spread hand. It was different from a lion track, yet I could not distinguish just what the difference was. Pepe, who had accompanied us to carry the rifles and game, pointed to the track and said vehemently:

"Tigre!" He pronounced it "tee-ger-ee." And he added, *"Grande!"*

"Big he certainly is," I replied. "Boys, we'll kill this jaguar. We'll bait this drinking trail with a deer carcass and watch to-night."

THE LAST FLOP

"TAKE THE HOOK OUT AND LET HIM GO," SAID R. C.

Once upon the bank, I was surprised to see a wide stretch of comparatively flat land. It was covered with a low vegetation, with here and there palm trees on the little ridges, and bamboo clumps down in the swales. Beyond the flat rose the dark line of dense jungle. It was not clear to me why that low piece of ground was not over-grown with the matted thickets and vines and big trees characteristic of other parts of the jungle.

We struck into one of the trails and had not gone a hundred paces when we espied a herd of deer. The grass and low bushes almost covered them. George handed his shotgun to Pepe and took his rifle.

"Shoot low," I said.

George pulled the trigger, and with the report a deer went down, but it was not the one I was looking at, nor the one at which I was sure he had aimed. The rest of the herd bounded away to disappear in a swale. Wading through bushes and grass, we found George's quarry, a small deer weighing perhaps sixty pounds. Pepe carried it over to the trail, and then joined us. I noted that he was exceedingly happy to carry the rifles and to be with us. We went on at random, somehow feeling that, no matter what direction we took, we would run into something at which to shoot.

And the first bamboo swale was alive with chicalocki. Up to this time I had not seen this beautiful pheasant fly in the open, and I was astonished at its speed. It would burst out of the thick bamboo, whirl its wings swiftly, then sail. That sail was a most graceful thing to see. George pulled his sixteen-gauge twice and missed both times. He had the beginner's fault—shooting too soon. Presently Pepe beat a big cock chicalocki out of the bush. He made

such a fine target, he sailed so evenly, that I simply looked
at him over the gun sights, and followed him till he was
out of sight.   The next one I dropped like a plummet.
Shooting chicalocki was too easy, I decided; they presented
so fair a mark that it was unfair to pull on them.

George was an impetuous hunter.   I could not keep near
him, or coax or command him to stay near me.   He would
wander off by himself.   That was one mark in his favor;
at least he had no fear.   Pepe hung close to me, with his
dark eyes roving everywhere; but I did not need his
cautious manner to make me alive to possibilities.   I
climbed out on one side of the swale, George on the other.
Catching his whistle, I turned to look after him.   He
waved and, pointing ahead, began to stoop and slip along
from bush to bush.   Presently a flock of Muscovy ducks
rose before him, sailed a few rods and alighted.   Then from
right under his feet labored up great gray birds.   Wild
geese!   I recognized them as George's gun went—bang!
One tumbled over; the others wheeled toward the river.   I
started down into the swale to cross to where George was,
when Pepe touched my arm.

"Turkeys!" he whispered.

That changed my mind.   Pepe pointed into the low
bushes ahead of me, and slowly led me forward.   I heard
a peculiar low thumping.   Trails led everywhither, and here
and there were open patches covered with a scant growth
of grass.   Across one of these flashed a bronze streak, then
another—and another.

"Shoot!   Shoot!" whispered Pepe, tensely.

Those bronze streaks were running turkeys.   The
thumpings were made by their rapidly moving feet.

"Don't they flush—fly?"   I queried of Pepe.

"No—no—shoot!" exclaimed he, as another streak of brown crossed an open spot. I hurriedly unbreeched my gun and changed the light shells for others loaded with heavy shot. We reached the edge of a bare spot across which a turkey ran with incredible swiftness. I did not get the gun in line with him at all. Then two more broke out of the bushes. Run! They were as swift as light. I took two snap shots and missed both times. If any one had told me it was possible for me to miss a running turkey at fifty feet I would have laughed at him. But I did not fetch a feather. Loading again, I yelled for George.

"Hey, George—turkeys!"

He whooped and started for us on the run. Just then there was a roar in the bushes and a brown blur arose and whizzed ahead like a huge bullet. That turkey had flushed. I watched him fly till he went down out of sight into a distant swale. There was another roar—a huge bronze cannon ball sped straight ahead—shot both barrels, and scored a clean miss. I watched this turkey fly and I saw him clearer. Then I was constrained to admit that the wild turkey of this Taumaulipas jungle had a swifter and more beautiful flight than my favorite bird, the ruffed grouse.

George came puffing up, gun in one hand, a heavy goose in the other.

"Walk faster," he said, "they'll flush better."

We hurried along, crashing through the bushes. I saw turkey after turkey. Bang! went George's gun. Then a beautiful sight made me cry out and almost forget my own gun. Six turkeys darted across an open patch—how swiftly they ran!—and rose in a bunch.

The roar they made, the wonderfully rapid action of their powerful wings, and then the size of them, their wildness and noble gameness, made them, at once and forever, the royal birds for me.

At the next threshing in the bushes my gun was leveled —I covered the whistling bronze thing that shot up—the turkey went down with a crash. Pepe yelled, and as I ran forward all the air about me was full of fine bronze feathers. I found my bird, wings wide stretched. Its strength and symmetry, and especially the beautiful shades of bronze, captivated my eye.

"Come on, boys—this is the greatest game I ever hunted," I called.

Again Pepe yelled, and this time he pointed. From where I stood I could see nothing but the low green bushes. George threw up his gun and shot. I heard a squealing.

"*Javelin! Javelin!*" called Pepe, in piercing tones.

George jerked a rifle from him and began to shoot. The trampling of hard little hoofs and a cloud of dust warned me where the *javelin* were. Suddenly Pepe broke and fled toward the river.

"Hyar, Pepe, fetch back my rifle!" I shouted, angrily.

George turned and dashed away, yelling: "Wild pigs! Wild pigs!"

It looked as if there was nothing else for me but to make tracks from that vicinity. Never before had I run from a danger which I had not seen, but the flight of the boys was irresistibly contagious, and this, coupled with the many stories I had heard of the *javelin*, made me execute a sprint that would have been a record but for the hampering weight of gun and turkey. I vowed I would hold on to both, pigs or no pigs; nevertheless, I listened as I ran and nervously looked back often. It may have been excited imagination that the dust cloud appeared to be traveling

CASTING NET FOR MULLET BAIT

in my wake. Fortunately, the distance to the river did not exceed a short quarter of a mile. Hot, winded, and thoroughly disgusted with myself, I halted on the bank. Pepe was already in the boat and George was scrambling aboard.

"A fine—chase—you've given—me," I panted. "There's nothing—after us."

"Don't you fool yourself," returned George, quickly. "I saw those pigs and, like the ass I am, I blazed away at one with my shotgun."

"Did he run at you? That's what I want to know!"

George said he was not certain about that, but declared there always was danger if a wounded *javelin* squealed. Pepe had little to say; he refused to go back after the deer we had left in the trail. So we rowed across the shoal, and on the way passed within a rod of an alligator. Had I not prevented George he would have wasted some more ammunition.

We reached camp tired out, and all of us a little ruffled in temper, which certainly was not eased by the discovery that we were covered with ticks. Following the cue of my companions, I hurriedly stripped off my clothes and hung them where they could singe over the campfire. There were broad red bands of *pinilius* round both my ankles, and reddish patches on the skin of my arms. Here and there were black spots about the size of my little finger nail, and these were *garrapatoes*. I picked these off one by one, rather surprised to find them come off so easily. Suddenly I jumped straight up with a pain as fierce as if it had been a puncture from a red hot wire.

Pepe grinned and George cried:

"Aha! that was a *garrapato* bite, that was! You just wait!"

George had a hundred or more of the big black ticks upon him, and he was remorselessly popping them with his cigarette. Some of them were biting him, too, judging from the way he flinched. Pepe had attached to himself a million or more of the *pinilius,* but very few of the larger pests. He generously came to my assistance. I was trying to pull off the *garrapato* that had bitten a hole in me. Pepe made me desist, saying it had imbedded its head and if pulled would come apart, leaving the head buried in the flesh, which would cause inflammation. Pepe held the glowing end of his cigarette close over the tick, and it began to squirm and pull out its head. When it was free of the flesh Pepe suddenly touched it with the cigarette and it exploded with a pop. A difficult question was—which hurt me more, the burn from the cigarette or the bite of the tick? Pepe scraped off as many of the *pinilius* as would come, and then rubbed me with *cañu,* the native alcohol. If this was not some kind of a vitriol I missed my guess. It smarted so keenly I thought my skin was peeling off. Presently, however, the smarting subsided, and so did the ticks.

We lounged about camp, resting in the shade during the hot midday hours. For supper we had a superfluity of meat, the waste of which I deplored, and assuaged my conscience by deciding to have a taste of each kind. The wild turkey I found the most toothsome, delicious meat it had ever been my pleasure to eat. What struck me at once was the flavor, and I could not understand it until Pepe explained that the jungle turkey lived upon a red pepper. So the

Taumaulipas wild turkey turned out to be doubly the finest game I had ever shot.

All afternoon the big alligator sunned himself on the surface of the shoal. I wanted an alligator skin and this was a tempting opportunity to get one, but I resisted it. Before sundown Pepe went across the river and fetched the carcass of the deer down to the bar.

Twilight found us stationed at the lower end of the island, comfortably ambushed behind rocks. I placed George and Pepe some rods below my position. They had the thirty-two calibre rifle and my shotgun loaded with solid ounce balls.

I settled down for a long wait, some fifty yards from the deer carcass. A wonderful procession of wild fowl winged swift flight over my head. They flew very low. It was strange to note the difference in the sound of their flying. The cranes and herons softly swished the air; the teal and canvas-backs whirred by, and the great Muscovies whizzed like bullets.

When the first deer came down to drink it was almost dark, and when they left the moon was up, though obscured by clouds. Faint sounds rose from the other side of the island. I listened until my ears ached, but I could hear nothing on our side. Heavier clouds drifted over the moon. The deer carcass became indistinct and then faded entirely, and the bar itself grew vague. I was about to give up watching for that night when I heard a faint rustling below me. Following it came a grating or crunching of gravel.

Bright flares split the darkness—crack! crack! rang out George's rifle, then the heavy boom! boom! of the shotgun.

"There he is!" yelled George. "He's down—we got him! There's two! Look out!"

I caught the flash of a long gray body in the hazy gloom of the bar, and took a quick shot at it. The steel-jacketed bullet scattered the gravel and then hummed away over the bank. The gray body moved so fast I could just see it; nevertheless, I turned the little automatic loose and made the welkin ring.

VI

TIGRE

When the echoes of the shots died away the stillness seemed more profound than ever. No rustle in the brush or scuffle on the sand gave evidence of a wounded or dying jaguar. George and Pepe declared there were two tigers and that they had hit one. I walked out upon the stones till I could see the opposite bar, but was not rewarded by a sight of dead game. Thereupon we returned to camp, somewhat discouraged at our ill luck, but planning another night watch.

In the morning George complained that he did not feel well. I told him he had been eating too much fresh meat and that he had better be careful. Then I set off alone, crossed the river, and found that the deer carcass was gone. In the sand near where it had lain were plenty of cat tracks, but none of the big jaguar. Upon closer scrutiny I found the cat tracks to be those of a panther. He had half dragged, half carried the carcass up one of the steep trails, but from that point there was no further trace.

I struck out across the flat, intending to go as far as the

jungle. Turtledoves fluttered before me in numberless flocks. Far to one side I saw some Muscovy ducks rising, sailing a few rods, then alighting. This occurred several times before I understood what it meant. There was probably a large flock feeding on the flat, and the ones in the rear were continually flying to get ahead of those to the fore.

Several turkeys ran through the bushes before me, but as I was carrying my rifle I paid little heed to them. I kept a keen lookout for *javelin*. Two or three times I was tempted to turn off the trail into little bamboo hollows; this, however, owing to my repugnance for ticks, I did not do. Finally, as I neared the high moss-decked wall of the jungle, I came upon a runway leading through the bottom of a deep swale, and here I found tiger tracks. Farther down the swale, under a great cluster of bamboo, I saw the scattered bones of several deer. I was sure that in this spot the lord of the jungle had feasted more than once. It was an open hollow with the ground bare under the bamboos. The runway led on into the dense leafy jungle. I planned to bait that lair with a deer carcass and watch it during the late afternoon. First, it was necessary to get the deer. This might prove bothersome, for my hands and wrists were already sprinkled with *pinilius* and I certainly did not want to stay in the brush very long at a time. The ticks were making me nervous. I imagined I felt an itching all the time, and writhed inside my clothes.

"Well, bite, blame you!" I said, resignedly, and stepped into the low bushes and went up and out of the swale. I had scarcely got my head over the level when I espied a troop of deer within easy range. Before they saw or winded me I let drive. The one I had singled out fell over

sideways; the others bounded away. When I saw the work
of the soft-nose .351 bullet I no longer wondered at the
deer falling in his tracks.

"If I ever hit a *tigre* like that it will be all day with him,"
I commented. There were two things about hunting a
jaguar that I had been bidden to keep in mind—his fierce
aggressiveness and remarkable tenacity of life. These are
qualities that make game worthy of a hunter's steel. I
dragged the deer down into the bamboo swale and skinned
out a haunch. Next to the wild turkey meat, I liked
venison best, and I was glad of this as an excuse, for shooting these tame tropical deer somehow seemed murder to
me. I left the carcass in a favorable position, and then
hurried back to camp.

To my great relief, I had managed to escape bringing
any *garrapatoes* with me; it took me, however, a half hour
to rid myself of my collection of *pinilius*.

"Pepe, what's the difference between a *garrapato* and a
pinilius?" I asked.

"The big tick is the little one's mother," replied Pepe,
and then volunteered more interesting natural history for
my edification. Of course, I took Pepe's word for it.

There were only a few ticks up here in the uplands; down
along the Panuco River, where the cattle roamed, there
were millions in every square rod. The under side of every
leaf and blade of grass was red with ticks. The size of the
ticks depended upon whether or not they got a chance to
stick to a steer or any beast. If they could not suck blood
they could not grow, yet they appeared to live indefinitely.
The *pinilius* grew into a *garrapato,* and a *garrapato* bred
a hundred thousand *pinilius* within her body. Two singular
facts concerning these ticks were first, that instinct made

them crawl always upward, and secondly that they vanished from the earth during the season of summer rains.

With me it was as George had sagely predicted—the ticks would make it serious. I soaked my hunting suit of Duxbak in kerosene in the hope that this heroic method would enable me to spend at least a reasonable time hunting. Then I waited for the long, hot hours to pass. It was cool in the shade, but the sunlight resembled the heat of a fire. At last five o'clock came and I put on the damp suit. Soaked with the oil it was heavier and hotter than sealskin, and before I got across the river I was nearly roasted. The evening wind sprang up and the gusts were like blasts from a furnace. My body was bathed in perspiration; it ran down my wrists, over my hands, and wet the gun. This cure for ticks—if it were one—was worse than their bites. When I reached the shade of the bamboo swale it was none too soon for me. I threw off the coat, noticing as I did so that there were more ticks upon it than at any time before. The bottom of my trousers, too, had gathered an exceeding quantity. I brushed them off, muttering the while that I believed they liked kerosene and looked as if they were drinking it. I found it easy, however, to brush them off of the wet Duxbak, and soon composed myself to rest and watch.

The position I chose afforded a clear view of the bare space under the bamboos, and of the hollow where the runway disappeared in the jungle. The deer carcass, which lay as I had left it, was about a hundred feet from me. This seemed rather close, but I had to accept it, for if I had moved farther away I could not have commanded both points.

I sat with my back against a clump of bamboos, the little

rifle across my knees, and an extra clip of cartridges on the ground at my left. After taking that position I determined, if the tiger came, not to move out of my tracks, and to kill him. It is desirable for a hunter, when his quarry is dangerous, to make up his mind beforehand, if that be possible. I had ten powerful shells that I could shoot in ten seconds; and I would have been willing to face two jaguars. This, of course, was before I had been introduced to one.

The sun set and the wind died down. What a relief was the cooling shade! The little breeze that was left fortunately blew at right angles to the swale, so that there did not seem much danger of the tigre winding me down the jungle runway.

For long moments I was tense and alert. I listened till I thought I had almost lost the sense of hearing. The jungle leaves were whispering; the insects were humming. I had expected to hear myriads of birds and see processions of deer, and perhaps a drove of *javelin*. But if any living creatures ventured near me it was without my knowledge. The hour between sunset and twilight passed—a long wait; still I did not lose the feeling that something would happen. My faculties of alertness tired, however, and needed distraction. So I took stock of the big clump of bamboos under which lay the deer carcass. It was a remarkable growth, that gracefully drooping cluster of slender bamboo poles. I remembered that as a youngster I had often wondered where the long cane fishing poles came from. Here I counted one hundred and sixty-nine in a clump no bigger than a barrel. They were yellow in color with black bands, and they rose straight for a few yards, then began to lean out, to bend slightly, at last to

GATHERING SHELLS AT CAPE ROMANO

Z. G. AT THE ROD. TARPON TEN FEET IN AIR

droop with their abundance of spiked leaves. I was marveling at the beauty of these slender tips when a noise startled me.

All in an instant I was tense as strung whipcord. What it was that I heard puzzled me. After a moment I seemed to fix the sound as having been an expulsion of breath from some creature's lungs. Warily I glanced around, raising myself a little, and craning my neck. A deep growl made me whirl.

There stood a jaguar with head up and paw on the deer carcass. I felt perfectly cool, but I was astounded. Even as I cautiously edged the rifle over my knee I took in the beautiful creature's points. He was yellow, almost white, with black spots; he was short and stocky, with enormous stumpy legs. But it was his head that most amazed me. It seemed huge.

He opened his jaws in a threatening growl, and his long yellow fangs gleamed. Not hurried, nor yet slowly, I fired. I heard the bullet strike him as plainly as if I had hit him with a board. I saw the dust fly from his hide. He leaped straight up with a roar that shook my nerve. I felt cold and tight all over. When he came down, sprawled on all fours, I pulled the automatic again.

The bullet went through him, for this time I saw fur fly. He leaped at me with strange hoarse utterance. When he landed I shot again and knocked him flat. I thought he was done for, but he tumbled and wrestled about, scattering the dust and leaves. Two times more I fired, too hastily, too sure of him, and as good as missed.

It took two deliberate seconds to snap in the other clip and push down the rod that threw the shell into the barrel. In that interval he would have reached me, if he could have kept his sense of direction. But he zigzagged; he was hard hit, had lost his equilibrium.

Then he made a magnificent leap that landed him within twenty-five feet of me, and when he plunged down he rolled clear over. I shot him through and through yet he got up, wheezing blood, uttering a kind of bellow, and sprang again at me.

If ever I fought a panic it was then! For a single instant the rifle wobbled. I was sick. Then I steadied down, grimly realizing in a lightning flash that my life was at stake.

Once while he was in the air I pulled, twice while he was down. Ten feet from me he rose to his full height, pawing the air with great spread claws, coughing, bleeding, desperate, horrible. I shot him straight between the wide-spread paws.

With twisted body, staggering, and blowing bloody froth all over me, he lunged forward blindly and fell over into the hollow.

Then began a furious wrestling that I imagined was his death throes. I could not see him down among the leaves and vines. In a moment there was a cessation of the struggles; then a movement of the weeds showed me he was creeping toward the jungle.

I sat down to reload the clips. They were hard to manage even for a calm person, and now, in the reaction of that desperate situation, I was far from calm. The jaguar crept steadily away, as I could tell by the swaying weeds and branches. What wonderful vitality! I must have shot him all to pieces. At last my trembling fingers pushed home shells in the two clips, and once more I loaded the rifle. Then I drew a deep full breath and made a powerful effort at composure. I had shot big game, and game that dashed at a hunter when it was hurt. But this was a different experience. I would never entirely get over it. How close that jaguar had come to getting me was proved by his own blood which he had coughed into my face. I recalled that I had felt the wind of his great paw.

In a moment I was myself again and more determined than ever to have that beautiful spotted jaguar. So I hurried along the runway and entered the jungle. Beyond the edge, where the bushes made a dense thicket, it was dry forest with little green low down. The hollow gave place to a dry wash. I could not see the jaguar but I could hear him dragging himself through the brush, cracking sticks, shaking saplings.

Presently I ran across a bloody trail and followed it. Every little while I would stop to listen. When the wounded jaguar was still I waited until he started to move again. It was hard going. The brush was thick and had to be broken and crawled under or through. As I had left my coat behind, my shirt was soon torn to rags. I peered ahead with sharp eyes, expecting every minute to come in sight of the poor crippled beast. I wanted to put him out of his agony. So I kept on doggedly for what must have been a long time.

The first premonition I had of my carelessness was to note that the shadows were gathering in the jungle. It would soon be night. I must turn back while I had light enough to follow my back track out to the open. The second came in shape of a hot pain in my arm, as keen as if I had jagged it with a thorn. Holding it out I discovered, to my dismay, that it was spotted with *garrapatoes.*

At once I turned back, and if I thought again of the jaguar it was that I could come after him the next day, or send Pepe. Another vicious bite, this time on my leg, confirmed my suspicions that many of the ticks had been on me long enough to begin their nefarious business. Then I was bitten in several places. Those bites were as hot as the touch of a live coal, yet they made me break out in a dripping cold sweat. It was imperative that I get back to camp without losing a moment which could be saved. From a rapid walk I fell into a trot. I got off my back-trail and had to hunt for it. Every time a tick bit me I jumped as if stung. The worst of it was that I knew I was collecting more *garrapatoes* with almost every step. When I grasped a dead branch to push it out of my way I could feel the ticks stick to my hand. Then I would whip my arm in the air, flinging some of them off to patter on the dry ground. Impossible as it was to run through that matted jungle I almost accomplished it. When I got out into the open, I did run, not even stopping for my coat, and I crossed the flat at top speed.

It was almost dark when I reached the river bank and dashed down to frighten a herd of deer. I waded the narrowest part of the shoal, and running up the island, burst into the bright circle of camp fire. Pepe and George jumped up with exclamations of fright. I was so choked up and breathless that at first I could not speak. My ragged, sleeveless shirt I threw into the fire, and then jerked off the rest of my clothes. In the bright glare I saw my arms black with *garrapatoes* and a sprinkling of black dots over the rest of my body. I was in agony.

"Boys, hurry, get busy," I said, with grim effort at endurance.

THE FUN OF FIGHTING SMALL FISH

Z. G. HOOKS BIG TARPON ON LIGHT TACKLE

It was well for me that I had a native like Pepe with me. First he dashed a bucket of cold water over me. How welcome it was! Then he told me to point out the ticks that were deepest—biting the hardest, he explained. I thought I was being eaten alive; it seemed impossible to segregate any particular stabs. But anything is possible with the mind. By absolute concentration on the pain I was enduring I was able to locate the most severe points.

Then the red-hot cigarette tips scorched my skin. That was the most trying ordeal of all my hunting days, or any other days. Pepe smoked and wore out three cigarettes, and George two, before they had popped all the biting ticks.

Then I was still covered with them. Pepe bathed me in *cañu*, which was a bath of fire, and soon removed them all. I felt flayed alive, peeled of my skin, and sprinkled with fiery sparks. When I had gotten into my pajamas and lain down, I was as weak as a sick cat. Pepe said the *cañu* would take away the sting very soon, but it was some time before I was resting easily.

VII

GEORGE'S JAGUAR

NEXT morning George again complained of not feeling very well, and he looked grouchy. He growled around camp in a way that might have nettled me, but having had ten hours of undisturbed sleep, I could not have found fault with anybody. I had expected to be sick, and here I was feeling fine.

"Come out of it, *Garrapato* George," I said. "Cheer up. Why don't you take *Pinilius* Pepe as gun-bearer and go out to shoot something? You haven't used up much ammunition yet—not more than a barrel."

My sarcasm was not lost on George.

"Well, if I do go I'll not come chasing in without some game."

"My boy," I replied, genially, "if you should happen to turn a corner and run face to face with a jaguar you'd— you'd let out one squawk and then never touch even the high places of the jungle. You'd take that crazy thirty-two rifle for a golf stick."

"Would I?" returned George, belligerently. "All right. Now you watch me!"

I did watch George awhile that morning. He performed a lot of tricks around camp. For one, he bounced bullets off the water in a vain effort to locate the anatomy of our basking alligator. For another, he tried his hand at fishing once more. He could get more bites than any fisherman I ever saw, but he could not catch anything. By and by the heat made me drowsy and I stretched myself on a blanket in the shade, and I bethought myself of a scheme to get rid of my noisy comrades for a while.

"George, take my hammerless and have Pepe row you along the shady bank of the river," I suggested. "Go sneaking along now and you'll get some shots."

He fell in with this idea, and Pepe, too, looked pleased. They got into the boat and were in the act of starting when George jumped ashore. He reached for his thirty-two and threw the lever down to see if there was a shell in the chamber. Then he proceeded to fill his pockets with ammunition.

"I might need a rifle," he said. "You can't tell what you're going to see in this darned jungle."

Whereupon he went aboard again and Pepe rowed leisurely upstream.

"Be careful, boys," I called, and composed myself for a nap. I promptly fell asleep. How long I slept I had no idea, and when I awoke I lay with languor, not knowing on the moment what had awakened me. Presently I heard a shout, then a rifle-shot. Sitting up, I saw the boat some two hundred yards above me, drifting along at about the edge of the shade. Pepe was in it alone. He appeared to be excited, for he laid down an oar to pick up a gun, and then reversed the performance. Also he was jabbering to George, who evidently was out on the bank, but invisible to me.

"Hey, Pepe!" I yelled, "what 're you doing?"

Strange to note, Pepe did not reply or even turn my way.

"Now where in the deuce is George?" I said, impatiently.

The hollow crack of George's thirty-two was a reply to my question. I heard the singing of a bullet. Suddenly, "spou!" it twanged on a branch not twenty feet over my head, and then went whining away. I heard it tick a few leaves or twigs. There was not any languor in the alacrity with which I put the big cypress tree between me and upstream. Then I ventured to peep forth.

"Look out where you're slinging lead!" I yelled. I doubted not that George had treed a black squirrel or was pegging away at parrots. Yet Pepe's motion appeared to carry a good deal of feeling—too much, I thought, presently, for small game. So I began to wake up thoroughly. I lost sight of Pepe behind a low branch of a tree that leaned out some fifty yards above the island.

Then I saw him again. He was poling with an oar, evidently trying to go up or down—I could not tell which.

Spang—spang! George's thirty-two spoke twice more, and the bullets both struck in the middle of the stream and ricocheted into the far bank with little thuds.

Something prompted me to reach for my automatic, snap the clip in tight, and push in the safety. At the same time I muttered George's words, "You can never tell what's coming off in this darned jungle."

Then, peeping out from behind the cypress, I watched the boat drift downstream. Pepe had stopped poling and was looking closely into the thick grass and vines of the bank. I heard his voice, but could not tell what he said. I watched keenly for some sight of George. The moments passed, the boat drifted, and I began to think there was nothing unusual afoot. In this interval Pepe drifted within seventy-five yards of where I knelt. Again I called to ask him what George was stalking, and this time Pepe said he did not know, but he did know that the animal was big. Hard upon this came George's sharp voice:

"Look out there on the island. Get behind something, for I'll be shooting that way. I've got him between the river and the flat. He's in this strip of shore brush. There!"

Spang! Spang! Spang!

Bullets hummed and whistled all about the island. I was afraid to peep out with even one eye. I began to fancy that we were playing Indians.

"Fine, Georgie! You're doing great!" I shouted. "You couldn't come any closer to me if you were aiming at me. What is it?"

Then a crashing of brush and a flash of yellow low down along the bank changed the aspect of the situation.

"Panther—or jaguar!" I ejaculated, in amaze. In a second I was tight-muscled, cold, and clear-witted. At that instant I discerned George's white shirt about the top of the brush.

"Go back! Get out in the open!" I ordered. "Do you hear me?"

"Where is he, Pepe?" shouted George, paying not the slightest attention to me.

I jumped from behind the tree and, running to the head of the island, I knelt low near the water with my rifle ready.

"*Tigre! Tigre! Tigre!*" screamed Pepe, waving his arms, then pointing.

George crashed into the brush. I saw the leaves move— then a long yellow shape. With the quickness of thought and the aim of the wing-shot, I fired. From the brush rose a strange wild sound. George aimed at a shaking mass of grass and vines, but before he could fire a long, lean, ugly beast leaped straight out from the bank to drop into the water with a heavy souse. Like a man half scared to death, Pepe waved my double-barreled gun. Then the water split to let out a yellow head. It was almost in line with the boat. I dared not shoot.

"Kill him, Pepe! Kill him!" I yelled.

Pepe did not know how to hold a gun, let alone aim one. He got the stock under his chin, and pointing the gun, he evidently tried to fire. But the hammerless did not go off. Then Pepe fumbled at the safety catch, which he probably remembered seeing me use. The jaguar, swimming with difficulty, perhaps badly wounded, made right for the boat.

Pepe was standing on the seat. Awkwardly he aimed. Bang! He pulled both triggers. The recoil knocked him backward. The hammerless fell into the boat and Pepe's broad back hit the water; his bare muscular legs clung to the gunwale, and slipped loose.

He had missed the jaguar, for it kept on for the boat. Still I dared not shoot. What on earth was the matter with George? Then I saw him, standing in the brush, fussing over the thirty-two. Of course, at the critical moment something had gone wrong with the old rifle.

Pepe's head bobbed up just on the other side of the boat. The jaguar was scarcely twenty feet distant and in line with both boat and man. At that instant I saw, or fancied I saw, our friend the alligator show some few rods toward the middle of the river. There was a heavy swirl in the water, and I knew the alligator was in that pool somewhere. George was screaming. It was no wonder I felt my hair stiffen. I kept bawling: "Shoot, George! Hurry, Pepe! The alligator! Look out!"

Pepe grasped the gunwale of the boat just as it swung against the branches of the low-leaning tree. He vaulted rather than climbed aboard.

"Grab an oar, Pepe! Keep the jaguar in the water! Don't let him in the boat!"

But Pepe did not hear me. Nimbly he ran and grasped the branches of the tree and leaped up just as the jaguar flopped against the boat.

I had only a fleeting instant to get a bead on that yellow body, and before I could be sure of an aim the branch weighted with Pepe sagged down to hide boat and jaguar. From the coldness of fear for Pepe I shifted to heat over the peculiarly exasperating situation.

Then George began to yell and shoot.

Spang! Spang! Spang! Spang!

"You idiot!" I roared. "You'll sink the boat!"

But a little thing like that did not matter to George. He stood up on the bank and worked the lever of his thirty-two with wild haste. The spat of the bullets could be heard plainly, and the sound was that of contact of lead and wood. So I inferred he was not hitting the jaguar.

Meanwhile Pepe had worked up from the lower end of the branch, and as soon as he straddled it and hunched himself nearer shore the leaves rose out of the water, exposing the boat. George saw the jaguar, for he kept shooting, but I could not see it. Then the boat swung loose from the branch and, drifting with the current, gradually approached the shore.

"Keep cool, George," I called, "we've got him now."

"He's mine! He's mine! Don't you dare shoot! I got him," howled George, in frantic excitement.

"All right. But steady up, can't you? Hit him once, anyway."

Apparently without aim, George fired, then, spasmodically working the lever, he fired again. The boat drifted into overhanging vines. Once more I saw a yellow-and-black object, then a trembling trail of leaves.

"Run back up the bank! He's coming out below you!" I yelled.

George disappeared. I saw no sign of the jaguar and heard no shot or shout from George. Pepe dropped from his branch down to the bank and caught the boat. I called him to come after me, and as soon as I had slipped on some clothes fit to hunt in I had him row me to the bank. I found the trail of the jaguar, followed it up to the edge of

the brush, and lost it on the flat. George was standing near.
He looked white and shaky and wild with disappointment.

"Oh, I had a dandy shot as he came out, but the blamed
gun jammed again. Come on, we'll get him. He's all
shot up. I bet I hit him ten times. He won't get away."

But an hour's useless stalking and searching served to
lessen his hope and augment his vexation. I finally got him
back to camp. The boat was half full of water, making it
necessary to pull it out on the bank and turn it over. There
were ten bullet holes in it.

"George, you hit the boat, anyhow," I said. "Now
we've a job on our hands."

So while I began to whittle pegs to pound into the bullet
holes, George wiped his flushed sweaty face and talked.

"We were up there a piece, round the bend. I saw a
black squirrel and went ashore to get him. But I couldn't
find him, and in kicking round in the brush I came into a
kind of trail or runway. Then I ran plumb into that darned
jaguar. I was so scared I couldn't remember my gun.
But the cat turned and ran. It was lucky he didn't make at
me. When I saw him run I got back my courage. I called
for Pepe to row downstream and keep a lookout. Then
I got out onto the flat. I must have come down a good
ways before I saw him. I shot and he dodged back into
the brush again. I fired into the moving bushes where he
was. And pretty soon I ventured to get in on the bank,
where I had a better chance. I guess it was about that
time that I heard you yell. . . . Then it all happened. You
hit him! Didn't you hear him? What a jump he made!
If it hadn't been so terrible when your hammerless kicked
Pepe overboard, I would have died laughing. Then I was
paralyzed when the jaguar swam for the boat. He was

hurt, for the water was bloody. Things came off quick, I tell you. Like a monkey Pepe scrambled into the tree. When I got my gun loaded the jaguar was clinging to the boat. Then I began to shoot. . . . I can't realize he got away from us. What was the reason you didn't knock him?"

"Well, you see, George, there were two fairly good reasons," I replied. "The first was that at that time I was busy dodging bullets from your rifle. And the second was that you threatened my life if I killed your jaguar."

"Did I get as nutty as that? But it was pretty warm there for a little . . . Say, was he a big one? My eyes were so hazy I didn't see him clear."

"He wasn't big, not half as big as the one I lost yesterday. Yours was a long, wiry cuss like a panther, and mean-looking."

Pepe sat on the bank, and while he nursed his bruises he smoked. Once he made a speech that was untranslatable, but I gave it an interpretation which was probably near correct.

"That's right, Pepe. We're pretty punk *tigre* hunters—*mucha* punk!"

VIII

CROCODILES

THAT night my dreams were not pleasant. I awoke from one in a fright and had no small task to persuade myself that half of my anatomy had not been chewed off by huge crawling black things.

It must have been late in the night, for the moon was low, and I was falling asleep again when the clink of tin pans made me sit up with a start. Some animal was prowling about camp. I peered into the moonlight shadows, but could make out no unfamiliar object. Still I was not satisfied, so I awoke Pepe and told him to get up and help me chase away the night marauders.

Certainly it was not my intention to let Pepe get out ahead of me and to take any possible risks; nevertheless, I was tired and slow, and Pepe rolled out of the tent before I had started.

"*Santa Maria!*" he shrieked.

I fumbled under my pillow for a gun. George raised up so quickly that he bumped my head, making me see a million stars.

From outside came a sliddery, rustling noise, then another yell that was deadened by a sounding splash. I leaped out with my gun, George at my elbow. Pepe stood just back of the tent, his arms upraised, and he appeared stunned. The water near the bank was boiling and bubbling; waves were dashing on the shore, and ripples spreading in a circle.

"Alligator!" I exclaimed, before Pepe had time to speak.

"*Si, si, Señor,*" replied he, and his big hands trembled. Then he said that when he stepped out of the tent the alligator was right in camp, not ten feet from where we lay. He also said that these brutes were man-eaters and that he would watch the rest of the night. I thought him, like all the natives, inclined to exaggerate; however, I made no objection to his holding watch. Nothing further happened to disturb our rest.

In the morning when I got up I viewed my body with curiosity. The ticks and the cigarettes had left me a beautifully tattooed specimen of aborigine. My body especially my arms, bore hundreds of little reddish scars— bites and burns together. There was not, however, any itching or irritation, for which I made sure I had to thank Pepe's skill and the *cañu*.

George did not get up when I called him. Thinking his sleep might have been broken, I let him alone a while longer, but when breakfast was smoking I gave him a prod. He rolled over, looking haggard and glum.

"I'm sick," he said.

My cheerfulness left me, for I knew what sickness or injury did to a camping trip. George complained of aching bones, headache, and cramps, and showed a tongue with a yellow coating. I said he had eaten too much fresh meat, but Pepe, after seeing George vomit, called it a name that sounded like *"colenturus."*

"What's that?" I inquired.

"Tropic fever," replied George. "I've had it before."

For a while he was a very sick boy. I had a little medicine case, and from it I administered what I thought was best, and he grew easier presently and went to sleep. Then I dispatched Pepe to the bamboo swale to get my coat, while I sat down to deliberate on the situation.

Whatever way I viewed it, I always came back to the same thing—we must get out of the jungle, and as we could not go back, we must go on down the river and trust to luck. That was a bad enough proposition even if George had been well. It was then I had a subtle change of feeling; a shade of gloom seemed to pervade my spirit.

Pepe returned with my coat, and also a choice collection of ticks. He reported big jaguar tracks around the remains of the deer carcass I had left in the swale. If George had not required my attention I would have had another watch in the twilight. But I stayed in camp and had the satisfaction of seeing him very much better by bedtime. I forbade him, and Pepe, too, to drink any more unboiled water. In the morning George was well enough to walk; however, he appeared weak and shaky. I decided to break camp immediately.

By nine o'clock we were packed, and turning into the shady channel, soon were out in the sunlight and saying good-by to Cypress Island. At the moment I did not feel sorry to go, yet I knew that reaction would come to me by and by, and that Cypress Island would take its place in my memory as one more haunting, calling wild place.

We turned a curve to run under a rocky bluff from which came a muffled roar of rapids. A long projecting point of rock extended across the river, allowing the water to rush by only at a narrow mill-race channel close to the shore. It was a ticklish obstacle to get around. There was no possibility of lifting the boat over the bridge of rock, and the alternative was shooting the channel.

We got out upon the rocks, only to find that drifting the boat round the sharp point was out of the question, owing to a dangerously swift current. I tried the depth of the water—about four feet. Then I dragged the boat back a little distance and stepped into the river.

"Look! Look!" cried Pepe, pointing to the bank

About ten yards away was a bare shelf of mud, glistening with water and showing the deep tracks of an alligator. It was a slide and manifestly had just been vacated. The alligator tracks resembled the imprint of a giant's hand.

"Come out!" yelled George, and Pepe jabbered to his saints.

"We've got to go down this river," I replied, and I kept on wading till I got the boat in the current. I was frightened, of course, but I kept on despite that. The boat lurched into the channel, stern first, and I leaped up on the bow. We shot down with the speed of a toboggan, and the boat whirled before I could scramble to the oars. What was worse, an overhanging tree with dead snags left scarce room to pass beneath. I ducked to prevent being swept overboard, but one of the snags that brushed and scraped me ran under my belt and lifted me into the air. I grasped at the first thing I could lay hands on, which happened to be a box, but I could not hold to it because the boat threatened to go on, leaving me kicking in midair, holding up a box of potatoes. I clutched a gunwale, only to see the water swell dangerously over the edge. In angry impotence I loosened my hold. Then the snag broke, just in the nick of time, for in a second more the boat would have swept away from me. I fell across the bow, held on, and soon, to my satisfaction, drifted from under the threshing branches, where I got to the oars. Pepe and George walked round the ledge, and were all smiles when they reached me.

"Boys, it wasn't funny," I declared, soberly.

"I said it was coming to us," replied George, with a hint of his old humor.

There were rapids below, which I went at in the way men face obstacles in the wilderness, when the dominant and controlling thought is to get out. More than one high wave curled spitefully round Pepe's shoulders. We came to a fall where the river dropped a few feet straight down. As usual in such places, I sent the boys around to meet me below. George made a detour and Pepe jumped right off the ledge into a foot or more of water.

Used as I was becoming to Pepe's wild yell, the one he now pealed out sent a shiver over me. Before looking, I snatched my rifle from the boat, then leaped upon the ledge of rock.

Pepe appeared to be sailing out into the pool. But his feet were not moving. I had only an instant, but in that I saw under Pepe a long black swimming shape leaving a wake in the water. He had stepped upon an alligator. Suddenly he leaped to a dry stone, and the energy of his leap carried him into the river beyond. Like a flash he was out again, spouting water. I shot a magazine of shells at the alligator. He made a thunderous surge, churning up a slimy foam, then vanished in a pool.

"I guess it's alligator day," I said, changing the clip in my rifle. "I'll bet I made a hole in that one. Look out below, boys."

I shoved the boat over the ledge in line with Pepe, and it floated to him, while I picked my way around the rocky shore. We piled aboard again and proceeded on our journey. I cautioned the boys to avoid wading unless it was impossible, in which case to use care where they stepped. Pepe pointed now and then to huge bubbles breaking on the surface of the water, with the information that they were made by alligators.

From then on my hands were full. We struck swift water, where rapid after rapid, fall on fall, took us downhill at a rate that was grim gratification to me. Where the current was not rough, it yet had a five- or six-mile speed, and as we had no portages, and pounded through the corrugated rapids of big waves, we made by far the best time of the voyage. The hot hours passed, cool for us because we were always wet; the sun sank behind a bald hill; the wind ceased to whip the streamers of moss; and at last, in a gathering twilight, we halted at a wide, flat rock to make camp.

"Forty miles, if we made an inch!" I declared, and both the boys said more.

We built a fire, cooked our supper, and then, weary and silent, rolled into our blankets. Next morning the mists had not lifted from the river when we shoved off, determined to beat the record of yesterday. Difficulties beset us from the start; the highest waterfall of our trip, a leak in the boat; deep, short rapids; narrows with choppy waves, and a whirlpool where we turned round and round, seemingly unable to row out. Nor did we get out till Pepe lassoed a snag and pulled us out.

About noon we came to another narrow chute brawling down into a deep, foamy pool. Again I sent the boys around and backed the boat through. Either I was tired or careless, for I drifted too close to a half-submerged rock, and try as I might, at the last moment I could not avoid a collision. As the stern went hard at the rock I expected to break something, but was surprised at the soft thud with which I struck. It flashed into my mind that the rock was moss-covered. Quick as the thought followed a rumble under the boat, the stern heaved up; there was a great sheet-like splash, and then a blow that splintered the gunwale. The boat shunted off, affording me a good view of a very angry eight-foot alligator. I had a clear view of him at close range. Manifestly he had been sleeping on the rock when I disturbed him. It was this look at him that enabled me to make a discovery. Instead of the wide rounded nose of the alligator he had the sharp nose and narrow jaws of the crocodile.

"Hey, George, that was a crocodile!" I shouted. "These devils are not alligators at all—they're crocodiles!"

"Same thing," replied George, laconically.

"Well, my boy, not so you'd notice it," I added. "I'll tell you something——"

"Say, the boat's half full of water; the gunwale's all split up," interrupted he.

We unloaded, turned out the water, broke up a box to use for repairs, and mended the damaged gunwale—work that lost us more than a good hour. Once more under way, we made some interesting observations. The river ceased to stand on end in places; crocodiles slipped off of every muddy promontory, and wide trails ridged the steep clay banks.

"Cattle trails, Pepe says," remarked George. "Wild cattle roam all over the jungle along the Panuco."

It was a well known fact that the rancheros of Tamaulipas State had no idea how many cattle they owned. I was so eager to see if Pepe had been correct that I went ashore, to find the trails were indeed those of cattle.

"Then, Pepe, we must be somewhere near the Panuco River," I said.

"*Quien sabe,*" rejoined he, quietly.

When we rounded the next curve we came upon a herd of cattle. They clattered up the bank, raising a cloud of dust.

"Wilder than deer," I exclaimed.

From that point conditions along the river changed. The banks were no longer green; the beautiful cypresses gave place to other trees, as huge, as moss-wound, but more

SECOND LEAP. NOTE THE BAIT SLIDING UP LEADER

TARPON LEAPING TOO CLOSE FOR COMFORT. BIG TARPON HAVE SMASHED SKIFFS AND KILLED ANGLERS

rugged and of gaunt outline; the flowers and vines and shady nooks disappeared. Everywhere wild wide-horned steers and cows plunged up the banks. Everywhere buzzards rose from grewsome feasts. The shore was lined with dead cattle and the stench of putrefying flesh was almost unbearable. We passed cattle mired in the mud, being slowly tortured to death by flies and hunger; we passed cattle that had slipped off steep banks and could not get back, and were bellowing dismally; and also we passed strangely acting cattle that Pepe said had gone crazy from ticks in their ears. I would have put these miserable beasts out of their misery had not George restrained me with a few words about Mexican law.

With all this I sickened, and though I drove the feeling from me, it continually returned. George lay flat on the canvas, shaded with a couple of palm leaves; Pepe rowed on and on, growing more and more into a settled quiet. His quick, responsive smile was wanting now. By way of a diversion, and also in the hope of securing a skin, I began to shoot at the crocodiles. George came out of his lethargy and took up his rifle. He would have had to be ill indeed to forswear any possible shooting; and now that I had removed the bar, he forgot he had fever. Every hundred yards or so we would come upon a crocodile, measuring somewhere from six feet on, and occasionally we would see a great yellow one, as large as a log. Seldom did we get within good range of these huge fellows, and shooting from a moving boat was not easy. The smaller ones, however, allowed us to approach quite close. George bounced many a thirty-two bullet off the bank, but he never hit a crocodile. I allowed him to have the shots, for the fun of it, and besides, I was watching for a big one.

"George, that rifle of yours is loaded. It doesn't shoot where you aim."

When we got unusually close to a small crocodile George verified my statement by missing his game by some yards. He promptly threw the worn-out rifle overboard, an act that caused Pepe much concern.

Thereupon I proceeded to try my luck. Instructing Pepe to row about in the middle of the stream, I kept my eye on one shore, while George watched the other. Since my failure to kill the jaguar I had lost faith in the little automatic, and now I had a chance to find out what it really could do. I shot half a dozen small crocodiles, but they slipped off the bank before we could get ashore. This did not appear to be the fault of the rifle, for some of the reptiles were shot almost in two pieces. But I had yet to learn more about the tenacity of life of these water brutes. Several held still long enough for me to shoot them through, then with a plunge they went into the water, sinking at once in a bloody foam. I knew the bullets had penetrated, for we found large holes in the mud banks lined with bits of bloody skin and bone.

"There's one," said George, pointing. "Let's get closer, so we can grab him. He's got a good piece to go before he reaches the water."

Pepe rowed slowly along, guiding the boat a little nearer the shore. At forty feet the crocodile raised himself, standing on his short legs so that all but his tail was free of the ground. He opened his huge jaws, either in astonishment or to intimidate us, I imagined, and then I shot him straight down the throat. He flopped convulsively and started to slide and roll. When he reached the water he turned over on his back with his feet sticking up, resembling a huge frog. Pepe rowed hard to the shore, just as the crocodile with one last convulsion rolled off into deeper water. I reached over, grasped his foot, and was drawing him up when a sight of cold, glassy eyes and open fanged jaws made me let go. Then he sank in water where we could not touch bottom with an oar.

"Let's get one if it takes a week," declared George. The lad might be sick, but there was nothing wrong with his spirit. "Gee! Look there!" he exclaimed. "Oh, I guess it's a log. Too big!"

We had often been unable to tell the difference between a crocodile and a log of driftwood until it was too late. In this instance a long, dirty gray object lay upon a low bank. Despite its immense size, which certainly made the chances in favor of its being a log, I determined this time to be fooled on the right side. I had seen a dozen logs—as I thought—suddenly become animated and slip into the river.

"Hold steady, Pepe. I'll take a crack at that, just for luck."

The distance was about a hundred yards, a fine range for the little rifle. Resting on my knee, I sighted low, under the gray object, and pulled the trigger twice. There were two spats so close together as to be barely distinguishable. The log of driftwood leaped into life.

"It's a crocodile!" yelled George. "You hit—you hit! Gee! Will you listen to that?"

"Row hard, Pepe—pull!"

He bent to the oars and the boat flew shoreward.

The huge crocodile, opening yard-long jaws, snapped them shut with loud cracks. Then he beat the bank with his tail. It was as limber as a willow, but he seemed unable to move his central parts, his thick bulk where I had sent the two mushroom bullets. Whack! Whack! Whack! The sodden blows jarred pieces from the clay bank above him. Each blow was powerful enough to have stove in the planking of a ship. All at once he lunged upward and, falling over backward, slid down his runway into a few inches of water, where he stuck.

"Go in above him, Pepe," I shouted. "Here! What a monster!"

Deliberately, at scarce twenty feet, I shot the remaining four shells into the crocodile. The bullets tore through his horny hide and spouted up blood and muddy water. George and Pepe yelled, and I kept time with them. The terrible lashing tail swung back and forth almost too swiftly for the eye to catch. A deluge of mud and water descended upon us and weighed down the boat. George and I jumped out upon the bank to escape it. There we ran to and fro in aimless excitement. I still clutched my rifle, but I had no shells for it. George was absurd enough to fling a stone into the blood-tinged cloud of muddy froth and spray that hid the thrashing leviathan. Presently the commotion subsided enough for us to see the great crocodile lying half on his back with belly all torn and bloody, and huge claw-like hands pawing the air. He was edging, slipping off into deeper water.

"He'll get away! He'll get away!" cried George. "What 'll we do?"

I racked my brains and suddenly had an inspiration.

"Pepe, get your lasso! Rope him! Rope him! Hurry! He's slipping!"

Pepe snatched up his lariat and, without waiting to coil it, cast the loop. He caught one of the flippers, hauled

WADING UPSTREAM

MICAS FALLS

WORKING DOWNSTREAM

CAMP ON CYPRESS ISLAND

tight on it, just as the crocodile slipped out of sight off the muddy ledge. George and I ran to the boat and, grasping hold of the lasso with Pepe, we squared away and began to pull. Plain it was that the crocodile was not coming up so easily. We could not budge him.

"Hang on, boys!" I shouted. "It's a tug of war."

The lasso suddenly streaked out with a kind of twang. Crash! went Pepe into the bottom of the boat. I went sprawling into the mud, and George, who had the last hold, went to his knees, but valiantly clung to the slipping rope. Bounding up, I grasped it from him and wound it round the sharp nose of the bowsprit.

"Get in! Hustle!" I called, falling aboard. "You're always saying it's coming to us. Here's where!"

George had hardly got into the boat when the crocodile pulled us off shore, and away we went, sailing downstream.

"Whoop! All aboard for Panuco!" yelled George.

"Now, Pepe, you don't need to row any more—we've a water horse," I added.

But Pepe did not enter into the spirit of the occasion. He kept calling on the saints and crying, *"Mucha malo."* George and I, however, were hilarious. We had not yet had experience enough to know crocodiles.

Faster and faster we went. The water began to surge away from the bow and leave a gurgling wake behind the stern. Soon we reached the middle of the river, where the water was deepest, and the lasso went almost straight down.

I felt the stern of the boat gradually lifted, and then, in alarm, I saw the front end sinking in the water. The crocodile was hauling the bow under.

"Pepe—your machete! Cut the lasso!" I ordered, sharply.

Wildly Pepe searched under the seat and along the gunwales. He could not find the machete.

"Cut the rope!" I thundered. "Use a knife, the ax—anything—only cut it—cut it quick!"

Pepe could find nothing. Knife in hand, I leaped over his head, sprawled headlong over the trunk, and slashed the taut lasso just as the water began to roar into the boat. The bow bobbed up as a cork that had been under. But we had shipped six inches of water.

"Row ashore, Pepe. Steady there. Trim the boat, George."

We beached on a hard clay bank, and rested a little before unloading to turn out the water.

"*Grande!*" observed Pepe.

"Yes, he was big," I assented.

"I wonder what's going to happen to us next," added George.

IX

JAVELIN

PEPE's long years of *mozo* work rowing for the tarpon fishermen now stood us in good stead. All the hot hours of the day he bent steadily to the oars. Occasionally we came to rifts, but they presented no difficulty to our passage, being merely swift, shallow channels over sandy or gravelly bottom. The rocks and the rapids were things of the past.

What annoyed us now was the scarcity of camping sites. The muddy margins of the river, the steep banks, and the tick-infested forests offered few places where it was possible to rest, to say nothing of sleep. Every turn in the widening river gave us hope, which resulted in disappointment. We found consolation, however, in the fact that every turn and every hour put us so much farther on our way. About five o'clock we had unexpected good fortune in the shape of a small sand bar, cut off from the mainland, and therefore free of cattle tracks. It was clean and dry, with a pile of driftwood at one end. Here we pitched camp.

But for the sense of foreboding in my mind, the vague feeling that all was not well with us, that we should hurry, hurry, hurry, I should have recovered my former cheerful spirits. George seemed to be holding his own, and Pepe's brooding quiet had at least grown no more noticeable, still I could not rid myself of a shade of gloom. If I had answered the question that knocked at my mind, instead of fighting it off, I should have admitted the certainty of disaster. So I kept myself busy at all kinds of tasks, and when there was no more for that day I watched the flight of wild fowl.

The farther down the river we traveled, the more numerous were the ducks and herons and cranes. But I saw no more of the beautiful *Pato Real,* as Pepe called them, or the little russet-colored ducks, or the dismal-voiced bitterns. On the other hand, wild geese and canvas-backs had become common and there were flocks of teal.

Pepe cooked duck, as usual, but George had lost his taste for meat and I made a frugal meal of rice. "Boys, the less you eat from now on, the better for you." It took resolution to drink the cocoa, for I could not banish thought of the green water and the shore line of dead and decaying

cattle. Still, I was parched with thirst; I had to drink.
That night we slept ten hours without turning over. Next
morning I had to shake Pepe to rouse him.

I took turns at the oars with Pepe. It was not only that
I fancied he was weakening and in need of an occasional
rest, but the fact that I wanted to be occupied, and especially to keep in good condition. We made thirty miles
by four o'clock, and most of it against a breeze. Not in
the whole distance did we pass half a dozen places fit for a
camp. Toward evening the river narrowed again, resembling somewhat the Santa Rosa of our earlier acquaintance. The magnificent dark forests crowded high on the
banks, always screened and curtained by gray moss, as if
to keep their secrets.

The sun was just tipping with gold the mossy crests of
a grove of giant cebias when we rounded a bend to come
upon the first ledge of rocks in two days. A low, grassy
promontory invited the eyes searching for camping ground.
This spot appeared ideal; it certainly was beautiful. The
ledge jutted into the river, almost to the opposite shore,
forcing the water to rush through a rocky trough into a
great foamspotted pool below.

We could not pitch our tent because the stony ground
refused to admit stakes, so we laid the canvas flat. Pepe
lunged up the bank with his machete in search of firewood.
To my utmost delight I found a little spring of sweet water
trickling from the ledge, and by digging a hole was enabled to get a drink, the first good one in more than a
week.

A little later, as I was spreading my blankets, George
called my attention to shouts up in the woods.

"Pepe's treed something," I said. "Take your gun and hunt him up."

I went on making my bed and busying myself about camp, with little heed of George's departure. Presently, however, I was straightened up by unmistakable shouts of alarm. George and Pepe were yelling in unison, and, from the sound, appeared to be quite a distance away.

"What the deuce!" I ejaculated, snatching up my rifle. I snapped a clip into the magazine, and dropped several loaded clips and a box of extra shells into my coat pocket. After my adventure with the jaguar I had decided never again to find myself short of ammunition. Running up the sloping bank, I entered the forest, shouting for the boys. Answering cries came from in front of me and a little to the left. I could not make out what was said.

Save for drooping moss the forest was comparatively open, and at a hundred paces from the river bank were glades covered with thickets and long grass and short palm trees. The ground sloped upward quite perceptibly.

"Hey, boys, where are you?" I called.

Pepe's shrill yells mingled with George's shouts. At first their meaning was unintelligible, but after calling twice I got the drift.

"*Javelin!* Go back! *Javelin!* We're treed! Wild pigs! *Santa Maria!* Run for your life!"

This was certainly enlightening and rather embarrassing. I remembered the other time the boys had made me run and I grew hot under the collar.

"I'll be darned if I'll run!" I said in the pride of conceit and wounded vanity. Whereupon I began to climb the slope, stopping every few steps to listen and look. I wondered what had made Pepe go so far for firewood. Still, there was nothing but green wood all about me. Walking round a clump of seared and yellow palms that rustled in the breeze, I suddenly espied George's white shirt. He was in a scrubby sapling not fifteen feet from the ground. Then I discovered Pepe, perched in the forks of a cebia, high above the thickets and low shrubbery. I was scarcely more than a dozen rods from them, down the gradual slope, and both saw me at once.

"Run!—you Indian, run!" bawled George, waving his hands.

Pepe implored me to fly to save my precious life.

"What for, you darn fools? I don't see anything to run from," I shouted back. My temper had soured a little during the last few days.

"You'd better run or you'll have to climb," replied George. "Wild pigs! A thousand of 'em!"

"Where?"

"Right under us. There! Oh, if they see you! . . . Listen to this." He broke off a branch, trimmed it of leaves, and flung it down. I heard a low trampling roar of many hard little feet, brushings in the thicket, and cracking of twigs. As close as I was, however, I could not see a moving object. The dead grass and brush were several feet high, up to my waist in spots, and, though I changed position several times, no *javelin* did I see.

"You want to look out! Say, man, these are wild pigs— boars, I tell you! They'll kill you!" bellowed George.

"Are you going to stay up there all night?" I asked, sarcastically.

"We'll stay till they go away."

"All right, I'll scare them away," I replied, and suiting action to word I worked the automatic as fast as it would shoot, aiming into the thicket under George.

Of all the fool things a nettled hunter ever perpetrated that was the worst. A roar answered the echoes of the rifle, and it was a trampling roar, circling round the space bounded by the trees the boys were in. Nervously I clamped a fresh clip of shells into the rifle. Clouds of dust arose, and strange little squeals or grunts sounded seemingly at all points above me. Then the grass and bushes seemed to wave apart and be divided by gray streaks. They were everywhere.

"Run! Run!" shrieked George, high above the tumult.

For a thrilling instant I stood my ground and fired at the bobbing gray backs. But every break made in the ranks by the powerful shells filled in a flash. Before that vicious charge I wavered, then ran as if pursued by demons.

The way was downhill. I tripped, fell, rolled over and over, still clutching my rifle, rose with a bound and fled. The *javelin* had gained on me. They were at my heels. I ran like a deer. Then, seeing a low branch, I leaped for it, grasped it with one hand, and, crooking an elbow round it, swung with the old giant swing of athletic days.

Hardly before I knew how it had happened I was astride a dangerously swaying branch directly over a troop of brownish-gray, sharp-snouted, fiendish-eyed little peccaries.

Some were young and sleek, others were old and rough, some had little yellow teeth or tusks, and all pointed their sharp noses upward, as if expecting me to fall into their very mouths. Feeling safe once more, I loaded the rifle and began to kill the biggest, most vicious *javelin*. When

I had killed twelve in twelve shots, I saw that shooting a few would be of no avail.   There were hundreds, it seemed, and I had scarcely fifty shells left.   Moreover, the rifle barrel grew so hot that it burned my hands.   Hearing George's yell, I replied, somewhat sheepishly:

"I'm all right, George—only treed.   How're you?"

"Pigs all gone—they chased you.   Pepe thinks we can risk running."

"Don't take any chances," I yelled in answer to this.

In trying to find a more comfortable posture, so I could apply myself to an interesting study of my captors, I made the startling discovery that the branch which upheld me was splitting from the tree trunk.   My heart began to pound in my breast; then it went up into my throat.   Every move I made—for I had started to edge toward the tree— widened the little white split.

"Boys, my branch is breaking!"   I called, piercingly.

"Can't you get another?" returned George.

"No!   I daren't move!   Hurry, boys!   If you don't scare these brutes off I'm a goner!"

My eyes were riveted upon the gap where the branch was slowly separating from the tree trunk.   I glanced about me to see if I could not leap to another branch.   There was nothing near that would uphold me.   In desperation I resolved to drop my rifle, cautiously get to my feet upon the branch, and with one spring try to reach the tree.   When about to act upon this last chance I heard Pepe's shrill yell and a crashing in the brush.   Then followed the unmistakable roar and crackling of fire.   Pepe had fired the brush—no, he was making his way toward me, armed with a huge torch.

THE AUTHOR AND HIS INDIAN, PEPE

TIRED SAILFISH IN LAST LEAP

X

OUT OF THE WOODS

"PEPE, you'll fire the jungle!" I yelled, forgetting what was at stake. I had a horror of forest fire.

The *javelin* stirred uneasily, ran around under me, tumbling over one another. When Pepe burst into sight, holding before him long-stemmed palm leaves flaring in hissing flames, the whole pack of pigs bowled away into the forest at breakneck speed.

"By heaven! Pepe, it was a nervy trick." I leaped down, and the branch came with me. George ran to us, his face white, his eyes big. Behind him came a roar that I thought might be another drove of *javelin* till I saw the smoke and flame.

"Boys, the jungle's on fire. Run for the river."

In our hurry we miscalculated the location of the camp, and dashed out of the jungle over a steep bank, along the base of which we had to wade to reach the ledge. Pepe did not appear very much concerned for the burning jungle, and expressed his belief that the fire would not hurt anything but the ticks.

I kept watching the forest back of us as if I expected it to blow up like a powder mine. Nevertheless, I was agreeably disappointed. A cloud of smoke rolled westward; there was a frequent roaring of burning palms, but the forest fire was nothing such as I had feared.

"Boys, we'll have some roast pig to-morrow. I guess there's fire enough up there for that," I remarked.

Just before dark, when we were at supper, a swarm of black mosquitoes swooped upon us. Pepe could not have evinced more fear of angry snakes, and he began to pile green wood and leaves upon the camp fire to make heavy smoke. We finished our meal before they attacked us, and then there was nothing to do but fight. These mosquitoes were very large, black-bodied, with white-barred wings; their sting was as painful as that of a wasp. We went to bed, but it was only to get up again, for the pests could bite through two thicknesses of blanket. The only thing we could do was to sit or stand in the smoke of the camp fire. There we spent a wretched sleepless night, with the bloodthirsty mosquitoes humming about our ears like a swarm of bees. They did not go away till dawn.

We were all haggard and languid, but George's condition showed me the necessity for renewed efforts to get out of the jungle. Pepe appeared heavy and slow, and what was more alarming, he had lost his appetite. We made George a bed on the canvas in the bow of the boat, where he was soon sound asleep. Then Pepe and I took turns at the oars, making five miles an hour.

As on the day before, we glided under the shadows of the great moss-twined cypresses, along the muddy banks where crocodiles basked in the sun and gaunt cattle came down to drink. Once we turned a bushy point to startle a large flock of wild turkeys, perhaps thirty-five in number. They had been resting in the cool sand along the river. Some ran up the bank, a half dozen flew right over the boat, and most of them squatted down as if to evade detection. Thereafter turkeys and ducks and geese became so common as to be monotonous.

About one o'clock we passed a thatched bamboo and palm-leaf hut on the bank. Some naked little Indians ran like wild quail. A disheveled black head peeped out of a door, then swiftly vanished. From there on we met frequently with huts, and at three o'clock sighted a large one situated upon a high bluff. Upon rounding a bend we came suddenly upon an intersecting river. It was twice as large as the Santa Rosa, and flowed swiftly.

"Taumaulipas," said Pepe.

"This must be the beginning of the Panuco," I returned. "I see tarpon rolling. We must be getting somewhere."

George roused out of his sleep and sat up, as interested and pleased as we were. The Panuco River, here formed, was very wide and flowed swiftly over sand bars. The banks were so high that we could see only the tips of the trees. We beached at the foot of the trail below the large hut, and, with Pepe and me lending aid to George, we climbed the steep bluff.

We found a cleared space in which were several commodious huts, gardens and flowers, a grassy yard upon which little naked children were playing with tame deer, parrots screeching, and two very kindly disposed and wondering native women. Pepe engaged them in conversation and learned that the village of Panuco was two days and two nights distant by canoe. How many miles or kilometers we could not learn, or whether or not the canoes traveled steadily day and night. We spent an hour there, and were much refreshed by the hot milk and the chicken-and-rice soup with which we were served. The women would accept no pay, so we made them presents. Pepe and George wanted to stay there that night, but I was for hurrying on our way. So we embarked and made perhaps fifteen more miles before time to camp.

But there was no place to camp. The muddy banks were too narrow at the bottom, and too steep to climb to the top. So I bade Pepe and George find as comfortable places as they could on the boat, and I sat down to make a night of it at the oars; I preferred to risk the dangers of the river at night than spend miserable hours in the mud.

Twilight had scarcely waned into night when the boys were both deep in slumber. Then the strange, dense, tropical night settled down upon me. The oars were almost noiseless and the water gurgled softly from the bow. Overhead the expanse was dark blue with a few palpitating stars. The river was shrouded in gray gloom and the banks were lost in black obscurity. Great fireflies enhanced the darkness. I trusted a good deal to luck in the matter of going right, yet I kept my ear keen for the sound of quickening current, and turned every few strokes to peer sharply into the gloom. I seemed to have little sense of peril, for, though I hit submerged logs and stranded on bars, I kept on unmindful, and by and by lost what anxiety I had felt. The strange wildness of the river at night, the gray veiled space into which I rowed unheeding, began to work upon my mind.

That was a night of nights. All that remained clear were the sounds and the smells, the feeling of the cool mist, the sight of long, dark forest line and a golden moon half hidden by clouds. Striking among these was the trill of river frogs. The trill of a Northern frog is music, but that of these great silver-throated jungle amphibians was more than music. Close at hand one would thrill me with mellow, rich notes, and then from afar would come the answer, a sweet high tenor, wilder than any other wilderness sound, long sustained, dying away till I held my breath to listen.

So the hours passed and the moon went down into the weird shadows and the Southern Cross rose pale and wonderful.

Gradually the stars vanished in a kind of brightening gray, and dawn was at hand. I awoke to the realization of weary arms and back. Morning came with its steely light on the river, the rolling and melting vapors, the flight of ducks and call of birds. The rosy sun brought no cheer this day. When we stopped, George did not leave the boat, and Pepe and I got breakfast in silence. Soon we were once more on the breast of the current.

I slept all the morning and awoke to find Pepe bowed over the oars. Watching him, I fancied he was stronger than on the preceding day, and I was relieved. We passed a long dugout canoe in which were two half naked natives poling with their huge paddles. Pepe's inquiry brought the information that we were two days from Panuco.

The river grew wider and long sand bars obstructed our passage. As it was quicksand we could not wade and had to pole off into the channels. This was wearisome work. We met another canoe and were told Panuco was far, far away, many kilometers. Towards night more natives informed us that the village was just around the next bend! I wondered dully whether this was their way of exercising a sense of humor. The stretches of the river were now miles long and the turns seemed interminably far apart. There was no village beyond any particular bend—nothing but bare banks for miles. We went ashore for a meager supper, rested a couple of hours, and about dark shoved off into the current.

I rowed until I gave out, then awakened Pepe. He took

the oars and I crawled back to the stern, where I covered my damp, chilly body with a blanket and fell asleep.

A rude hand brought me back from oblivion. Pepe was shouting in Spanish. I heard the soft swish of swift current. Raising myself, I caught the glimmer of glancing water under the lowering moon. Pepe was frantically pushing his oar into the stream in an effort to shove us off a sand bar. As we seemed solidly fixed and in no danger whatever, I calmed Pepe's fears, and we lay down in the boat and slept till morning.

That day was a repetition of the one before, except that it was hotter, wearier, and the stretches of river were longer, and the natives we met in canoes more stolidly ignorant of distance. The mourning of turtledoves almost drove me wild. There were miles and miles of willows, and every tree was full of melancholy doves. At dusk we halted on a sand bar, too tired to cook a dinner, and sprawled in the warm sand to sleep like logs.

In the morning we brightened a little, for surely just round the bend we would come to Panuco. Pepe rowed faithfully on, and bend after bend lured us with deceit. I was filled with weariness and disgust, so tired I could hardly lift my hand, so sleepy I could scarcely keep my eyes open. I hated the wide, glassy stretches of river and the muddy banks and dusty cattle.

At noon, when we came unexpectedly upon a cluster of thatched huts to find they made up the village of Panuco, I was sick, for I had expected a little town where we could get some drinking water, and hire a launch to speed us down to Tampico. This appeared little more than other places we had passed, and I climbed up the bank wearily thinking of the long fifty miles we still had to go.

But Panuco was bigger and better than it looked from the river. We found a clean, comfortable inn where we dined well, and learned, to our joy, that a coach left in an hour for Tamos to meet the five o'clock train to Tampico.

We hired a *mozo* to row the boat to Tampico and, carrying our lighter things, we boarded the coach and behind six mules were soon bowling over a good level road.

It was then that the spirit of my mood changed. The gloom faded away as I had seen the mist clouds dissolve in the morning sunlight. It was the end of another wild trip, which I suddenly found had not been so bad after all. As rest from weary labor and assurance of a safe escape from the wilderness became certainties I began that strange and inevitable longing for another trip some day. That feeling grew with the hours and miles. When the little palm-thatched village of Tamos came in sight the sun was setting, and into the rose and golden sky a flock of flamingoes winged regular and beautiful flight, leaving me a thrilling reminder of the lonely jungle river.

THE END